How To Add Adventure To Your Life

The Seven Cs to Success

GW00499209

by John Peck

Praise for *The Seven Cs*

'As someone who has spent much of his life taking on great challenges, it is refreshing for me to see a fellow adventurer outline the many steps from the start of a dream to success. I believe *The Seven Cs* will prove extremely useful for anyone facing big choices or seeking new goals. Hats off to John Peck for producing a book that could have life-changing results, no matter what sort of adventure you seek.'

Sir Chris Bonington

'John Peck may appear to be just an exemplary adventurer in the traditional sense, with countless inspirational and motivational stories to tell, but he is so much more than that. His modest, self-deprecating demeanour belies an incredible depth of knowledge, experience, insight and capability. I like him, admire him and would honestly say he is one of the finest human beings I have ever met.

'As someone who has had some success and many failures in trying to live an adventurous life and achieve some extraordinary challenges, I can't recommend *The Seven Cs* highly enough. If I'd had this book earlier, I feel certain I'd have had many more successes and considerably fewer failures.

'I believe the best way of learning anything is to break it down into manageable chunks and take a step-by-step approach. John Peck's Seven Cs model does this perfectly. In my humble opinion it offers more than just practical knowledge – it contains real wisdom.'

Jonathan Blain,
author, thought leader, entrepreneur and adventurer

'I love the central concept of this book: that if your desire to achieve what you care about is strong enough, then your ability and your potential can be focused into an unstoppable power. John can orchestrate that alchemy time and time again for those he works with. Magic indeed!'

Alex Mahon, Channel 4 CEO

'John Peck's fascinating and insightful *Seven Cs* has its roots in the high-risk adventures he described in his first book, *Restless*. During his career as a motivational speaker and leadership coach, he has often been asked what methodology he used to decide if he ought to undertake a dangerous adventure. He realised there had been no blueprint that would have guided him, so he decided to create one. This book is the result.
'It spells out the seven areas of attributes and capabilities that he believes should be carefully considered before any high-risk challenge is tackled. Its principles and recommendations are as relevant to business challenges as they are to those undertaking adventures in the great outdoors. *The Seven Cs* is brimming with wisdom from experience and offers hard-earned advice on avoiding pitfalls.'

Major General Ian Freer CB CBE

'Written in John's easy style and with all his practical experiences brought to bear, this is a useful companion for anyone who wants to achieve more in life – at home, in business or in the world of adventure. The reader will be fired up and ready to go in no time.'

**Andrew Walters,
chairman of London Biggin Hill Airport**

'I greatly enjoyed reading John Peck's book on the Seven Cs model. It is an excellent guide to helping one prepare for the many challenges of life, drawing on examples from John's many exciting adventures.'

Captain Peter Voute CBE, Royal Navy

'Few of us have the courage to venture beyond the dream stage, so for those who want to challenge themselves with the adventure of a lifetime, or a new – and perhaps risky – business venture, *The Sevens Cs* is essential reading. John has repeatedly pushed the boundaries and his life is now a library of experience for others to draw upon. I am sure *The Seven Cs* will be a success because there are many who need the push to start the process of working towards their dream.'

**John Purnell GM QPM DL,
former deputy assistant commissioner Metropolitan Police,
and deputy lieutenant of Greater London**

Contents

First Published in Great Britain in 2022

Copyright © 2022 John Peck

A CIP catalogue record for this book is available from the British Library

ISBN 978-1-7395916-0-1 (print)

ISBN 978-1-7395916-1-8 (ebook)

Cover Design by Creative Covers
Typesetting by Book Polishers

Dedication

This book is dedicated to all those readers who have faced (or are facing) a moment of 'commitment' in life.

I imagine that many of you have already had to face down the four dragons: fear, anxiety, uncertainty and risk. I certainly have.

And some of you may even at this moment be trying to decide if now is the time to move forward with a major plan or if the smart thing to do is take a step back. My hope is that this book will help guide you in the right direction. And if there is something that you have always wanted to do – an adventure, a project, a new business – but did not even know where to start, or were fearful of doing so, this book is for you too.

My goal is not to drag you into a world of danger and reckless decisions. In these uncertain times, just getting on with life is a hard enough task in itself. But the ultimate goal for all of us, I guess, is twofold: managing the day-to-day challenges of living and, at the same time, finding ways of truly being 'alive'. That has always been my quest and this book describes the process that has taken me to where I am today on my continuing journey.

Whatever your goal, there will be obstacles to overcome, but the rewards will be great. If *The Seven Cs* inspires you to take your next big step – or your first – and helps you to navigate the choppy waters to come in a more confident, fulfilling and fruitful way, my task will be complete.

Pushing the Boundaries

John Peck has lived the kind of life that most of us can only dream of. He's rowed the Atlantic, walked to the North Pole, run across the Sahara and summited previously unclimbed Himalayan peaks. His has been a life of exploration, forever pushing his body and mind to their limits. When it comes to offering advice on adventure, there are few people more qualified than Mr Peck.

In his first book, *Restless*, John discussed some of the challenges that have shaped his life. Although these vary greatly in length, terrain and difficulty, uniting all of them is John's sense of curiosity for life-expanding experiences.

This seems to have been with John from the very early days. In *Restless*, he described how he felt after climbing Popocatépetl, an active volcano that stands at 17,802ft (5,426m) and is Mexico's second-highest peak: 'I had fallen in love with high-level climbing and the big peaks were beckoning me.'

These bigger peaks included an epic adventure up a Himalayan mountain known only as Peak 6529. Braving horrendous conditions and frostbite, and powered by tea and an unshakeable sense of purpose, John somehow made it to the summit. He logged that particular adventure in the file marked 'stretch experience'.

John has been equally stretched on the water. Indeed, one of his earliest voyages, a crossing of the Channel in 1975, led to one of the most famous RNLI rescues of the 20th century, when the boat he was in was caught in force 10 gales and 30-foot waves. Instead of being put off the water for life, John aimed higher. In 2004, accompanied by lifelong friend Fraser Dodds, he joined the select group of people to have rowed the Atlantic, becoming, at 58, the oldest Briton to make the 3,000-mile voyage.

Following that epic achievement, he completed the Marathon des Sables ultramarathon, a 156-mile race over seven days in the Sahara that is often described as the toughest footrace on the planet. Perhaps in a bid to cool off, he then walked to the North Pole.

In his capacity as a coach and public speaker, John has encouraged hundreds of people to take on adventures of their own – whether that's climbing a mountain, rowing across an ocean or simply becoming more confident in day-to-day life. Through his work with inner city gangs and people with addictions, John has used outdoor adventure to help rebuild and redirect lives. And his career as both an army officer and senior police officer has fostered in him an abiding sense of social responsibility and discipline that guides him to this day.

I've been fortunate enough to meet John several times and am always struck by his remarkable ability to galvanize people around a challenge. He makes the impossible seem possible – and he also makes it fun. I know this approach has helped to inform his Seven Cs model, as it places equal value on the qualities of imagination, passion and pragmatism. It's a toolkit for the aspiring adventurer and an insight into the working process of a man who's consistently taken something from a wild idea to a real-world accomplishment.

If you're looking to push back the barriers in your life, *The Seven Cs* will help to guide you on your voyage.

Rick Pearson, senior editor, Runner's World UK

Preface

A couple of years have gone by since I published my first book, *Restless,* in which I described the reality of taking on potentially dangerous and (for me) seemingly impossible challenges in remote landscapes.

I wrote about the experience of being trapped at high altitude on an unclimbed peak in the Himalayas; of trekking across the Sahara in the infamous Marathon des Sables ultramarathon; and of the nine and a half weeks spent rowing across the Atlantic Ocean in a small boat.

It was exciting to see that the book sparked interest not only in fellow adventurers but also in people who had never taken on such challenges. Many of them wrote to me and said how much it inspired them to tackle new goals with a courage and determination they did not know they had.

I was also lucky enough to be invited to give talks to large organisations, alongside working with smaller leadership groups, to help them find new ways to tackle the tough challenges they face at work and elsewhere in their lives. To give some sense of order to these adventure talks, I decided to try to put together a model people could take away that could help provide some memorable structure to the messages. I was further motivated by the question I was often asked at the end of a talk: 'But how do you go about making these adventures come to life?'

It was a good question. I'd always had an ability to turn an idea into a reality but couldn't put my finger on quite how I did it. Was there some process or pattern to my approach? If so, what was it?

One day, when trekking in the Brandberg mountain range in Namibia, Southern Africa, I decided to invest some time in working out exactly how this sequence took place. That's when the critical Seven Cs model started to come together in my mind.

My dream was to produce a path to success that would be as helpful to a young person starting out on a new business of their own as it would be to someone planning to climb a Himalayan peak. If a serious challenge is a bit like an iceberg – most of it cannot be seen from the surface – this book would have to focus on the hidden element.

Such a book, I knew, could not be made up of fancy management jargon (much as I would like it to be useful to business leaders taking on huge challenges). Rather, if the book – and the model it set forth – were to be useful to people in their everyday lives, it would have to match the reality of my experience.

And so, to create the model, I have looked back not only at my adventures, but also my experience of leadership as a young army officer and a senior police officer. This has allowed me to outline a pathway to success and, of equal importance, it means I can pinpoint moments when I fell off track.

For those of you who, quite reasonably, have no interest in stepping into the world of extreme adventure, I hope this book may still ignite some passion or desire in you to take on a challenge in your own life, however big or small. Some of the most rewarding feedback I get when I give talks on adventure is from self-described 'unadventurous' people. I cannot adequately convey the joy I feel when they tell me I have inspired them to take a brave step forward.

The Seven Cs model follows what I believe to be the typical path from taking something from 'idea to reality', but don't be tied to the order of the chapters. If you prefer a more random, less structured approach, feel free to dip into the book and head for any chapter that piques your interest.

Ultimately, if this book helps you to succeed in an endeavour that may once have felt beyond your abilities – or even encourages you to begin a new challenge – then I have done my job. I wish you luck in your journeys ahead.

John (July, 2022)

Introduction

Succeeding in uncertain times

What would I like to achieve with this book?

I have coached many people over the years who had set their sights on serious challenges, such as rowing across an ocean or dragging heavily laden 'pulks' (or sledges) unsupported to the North Pole. From my own explorations and the achievements of likeminded souls, I have learnt that there is a natural pathway to success and by following that route the journey feels far clearer and more logical. My task in coaching people has been to put the end game within their reach. My intention in this book is to reveal that pathway and open it up so others can take it.

What this book is not

This is definitely *not* a motivational book for people who want to give up smoking or lose weight. There are many other writers who cover these topics far better than I could.

It is also not a book to encourage the unwary to take on challenges that are out of their depth – that way lies disaster.

Nor is it a quick fix. I will not be telling people, 'All you have to do is to believe in something hard enough and success is inevitable.' Any challenging adventure requires serious planning

– and even then, it is likely to push you to your limit and throw up obstacles you could not have foreseen. If it was any easier, it wouldn't be an adventure and you wouldn't need this book.

Who is this book for?

Gender is irrelevant and so is age – some of my most adventurous undertakings happened as I reached my 60s.

You should have a natural aptitude for serious adventures and challenges, and a willingness to become physically fitter and mentally tougher than perhaps you have ever been.

You need to have reached a stage in your life where you can sense a call to adventure, even if you don't quite understand where that call is coming from or where it will take you.

And you need to have courage – or be up for testing and developing your courage again and again. This will help you to face up to real or potential danger in the field, but, far more than that, it will give you the strength, determination and confidence to ignore the people who will try to dissuade you from setting out on your adventure.

If you are itching for a way to challenge yourself, if you are someone who has a goal but does not know how to go about achieving it, if you believe that you can do more with your life, then this is the book you should be reading.

The Seven Cs: an overview

Before going into detail on each of the Seven Cs, here is a quick overview of what is to come. The chapters (the steps along the pathway) are in the order in which I think adventure planning tends to take place, but if a particular section of the model jumps out at you, feel free to start there and create your own order.

1. CARE

This is the key element in the model; it addresses the level of desire or passion that kicks off and underpins the project. If it is powerful enough, it will help to propel you through the other six stages. Without Care, all the other elements will feel so much harder and may be unattainable. At this early stage, your initial idea is not yet a goal – it remains more of a dream. If I were to compare it with falling in love, this is the moment when you look across the room, lock eyes with someone and are instantly smitten. You know that life will never be quite the same after this. You can't get the idea out of your mind, and it drives your thinking and your energies to a level that is thrilling but, as yet, may seem slightly irrational. I think the essence here is caring less about everything that everybody else thinks it is your duty to care about, and more about what it is that really excites you to the point of putting yourself on the line to get it. We will examine this moral dilemma later in the book, but in my experience, unless the dream is burning bright in you at the start, it will remain just that – a dream. This chapter will help you to discover what you truly care about.

2. CAPABLE

In the early stages of planning an adventure, you may have no idea whether you are capable, or could become capable, of achieving it. Part of the fun of the adventure is in finding out. However, by better understanding your strengths and weaknesses, you can begin to set and achieve challenges that truly stretch you. Many of us misjudge our capacity, often believing ourselves capable of much less than we truly are. Without encouraging recklessness, this chapter aims to help you break down the unhelpful thoughts and beliefs that are holding you back from achieving your true potential.

3. CURIOSITY

Humans are born with an innate sense of curiosity – but few of us develop it and even fewer have the courage to step outside their comfort zone and use it to their advantage. It is the fuel that will help you find new solutions, ideas and projects. This restless energy is the font of so much drive, adventure and achievement. It can also be dangerous and boundless amounts of it can be a real pain. In this chapter, we'll investigate things such as: how curious are you as a person? What is the level of your ingenuity? What lengths are you prepared to go to in order to find the information you need to get your project off the ground?

4. COMMIT

This is the moment you cast off the mooring ropes, pull up the anchor and set off into the unknown to find another shore. When I meet people who want to row across the Atlantic Ocean or drag sledges to the North Pole, I sense the power of the commitment that is running red hot through their veins. During the adventure-planning process, there comes a point when you have to commit and get on with the hard work, money worries, pain and general hardship that are part of pursuing anything worthwhile. Once on that path, there may be no going back. Just make sure that you don't commit because an overinflated ego has taken over. You are not making this commitment to prove something to others, to hear their applause or to compete with someone else – the only competition is with yourself and the ultimate commitment is to yourself.

5. CLARITY

This is the left-brain rational bit, where all the planning takes place and the 'what ifs' are considered. It's a time to review and take stock of what needs to be done to keep you on the path to success. There is no replacement for good, timely and accurate administration – and it's hard work. You'll need to be committed to research and scenario planning. This is when you'll lay the foundations for future success. This is also the chapter in which we'll look at gaining clarity as to why you are doing something. Having a clear, meaningful motivation for a challenge can make all the difference when things get tough.

6. CONNECT

Who do you need to connect with to get results? Do you plan to work solo or with a partner or a team? Who do you need to get involved? While self-reliance is an important quality in any adventurer, the willingness to draw on the strength of others is, arguably, even more crucial. And it is upon this latter quality – the ability to connect – that this chapter will concentrate. We'll look at the advantages of going solo versus going as a team, how to go about selecting the right people and the importance of asking for help when it's needed.

7. COURAGE

How are you going to keep sane and manage the strain to come? Do you have the courage to assert yourself, to persist in the pursuit of your dream when others rail against you? Do you have the wherewithal and the resilience to keep going when you are desperate to give up? Courage is one of the essential tools for survival when things get tough – and we often have more of it than we imagine. In this chapter, my aim is to show you how to find, foster and harness the courage that lives inside you – so that you can call upon it when the situation demands.

The power of the courage that waits inside you can be boosted using a range of techniques or 'Coping Strategies'. I have included a section in the appendix at the end of the book to illustrate how elite performers employ these strategies to get the most from themselves, particularly when they're under extreme pressure. And I'll show you how you can use them, too.

Chapter 1: CARE

What really excites you?

'The starting point of all achievement is desire. Keep this constantly in mind. Weak desire brings us weak results, just as a small fire makes a small amount of heat'

– Napoleon Hill, self-help guru and author

I believe it is precisely the depth of how much one *cares* about an idea that determines if a dream becomes a reality. At this stage of an adventure, the idea is just that: an idea. It is not yet even a goal, vision, mission or plan. That all comes later. Sometimes, the idea emerges from watching a film or reading a book. Sometimes, it is born out of a loose, excited conversation fuelled by a bottle of wine – or two. It is an exciting, giddy phase. Don't worry about rationale or logic at this point; for now, all you need to know is that the fire burns with enough strength to take you to the next part of the model. This chapter is designed to help you identify what you truly care about and harness your energy to turn an idea into a reality.

What Do You Care About?

A favourite exercise of mine when working with groups of people who are considering their futures is to invite them to think back to moments in their life when they were truly in a state of flow. These are the precious moments when everything seems to be in alignment.

If you are scratching your head, certain that these moments have not yet occurred in your life, do some future visioning – imagining a future with a new experience that will leave you truly fulfilled. This may be a seemingly crazy adventure, a professional goal or even putting yourself in service to others. The key thing about these moments is that they will arouse your passion and leave you energised and inspired.

Here, it is worth differentiating between extended periods of your life when things were running smoothly and those moments of excitement and achievement that left you with a real buzz. It is the latter that I have in mind here.

In the hurly-burly world of commitments, it is hard to find moments when you can feel truly fulfilled in the midst of an exciting challenge. With a little luck, it can happen through work, but, very often, these moments are created in an environment that is outside your day job.

They don't have to be complicated or require huge investment. For example, ideas often occur to me when sitting on the beach alone, watching the tide go back and forth, or running along the cliffs on a stunning piece of coastline, marvelling at the incredible views unfolding before me. It's at moments such as these when I feel truly at peace with the world.

Alternatively, I can remember times when I have been working to support someone who has been through a tough time and, suddenly, I can see them transforming and opening up to a whole new way of looking at life and the challenge they are trying so hard to deal with. These are the moments when I feel truly inspired.

Ultimately, what you care about is very often linked to the key values in your life. Whatever it is, when you are setting sail on a new adventure or challenge in your life, without the stardust of care, your mission will lack the personal imperative that will drive you forward when things get tough.

Perhaps the real question is: when you get to the end of your life and are looking back from the comfort of your rocking chair, will you have any regrets about missed opportunities? Will you be able to put your hand on your heart and be genuinely happy with what you have achieved, the risks you took and the challenges you overcame? Did you fulfil your dreams? That is what this chapter is all about.

The Big Picture

When faced with a bold new idea for the first time, there are often too many facets to take in. Indeed, with the most exciting ideas, it's not even worth thinking in much detail yet, as it would detract from the vitality, the essence and the attraction of the fundamental concept.

I've mentioned that finding and deciding to act upon a new

idea is akin to falling in love. Think of that heady moment when you were first intoxicated by the presence of another person.

So it has been for me with the adventurous projects I have undertaken. Very often they are sparked by a chance encounter, where somebody has mentioned a possibility that sounded truly exciting and, on occasion, out of reach.

From the moment I first hear of such a possibility, I can't get it out of my head – it's as though I have been bewitched by it. And so I would like to share with you the first in a number of secrets I have uncovered – sometimes stumbled across – in my many years of adventuring.

The Power Of Emotional Energy

With each new adventure, it is the build-up of emotional energy resulting from the initial idea that drives the pursuit. Consequently – and contrary to popular belief – in many cases it is the level of desire, not the level of ability, that determines success in adventure.

Consider some of the greatest leaders of our time – people such as Martin Luther King Jr and Nelson Mandela. They were consumed by a passion that went far beyond what might be considered normal. Their dream penetrated so deeply that they could not let it go.

Certainly, I have reached this point of decision on several of the more dangerous expeditions in which I have been involved: the point at which the level of belief is such that nothing will stop you but death itself. Such inextinguishable desire often ensures that the dream becomes a reality.

Do You Remember The First Time?

If you've been fortunate enough to have found love, think back to that first thunderbolt of intense attraction. Try to remember how you felt and, if possible, try to summon up the words to match those feelings. Not easy, is it? Words often seem inadequate to the task of describing a moment of such singular importance – this is strikingly similar to the way adventurers find themselves leaping forward to engage with an idea, blind to the possibility of failure and enraptured by the potential for success.

Let us at least try to put words to the feeling.

Firstly, there is a strong 'desire' for the other person, which acts as the impetus to win their heart. The words 'wish' and 'dream' can also apply, as they convey a sense of profound longing for what might be possible.

People in love – especially those in the early, euphoric stage of a relationship – often describe themselves as feeling 'restless' when they are not with the person who has turned their life upside down and come to occupy every waking thought. And so it is when an idea takes hold.

The Passion Prospect

What I find most interesting about the act of falling in love is not the ability to ascribe values or labels to it; instead, it is the very qualities that are impossible to name or pin down that make it so desirable. You can't truly understand the concept of being in love if you have not experienced it. Reading about it, seeing it in others, hearing about it – these are not enough. Only those who have fallen deeply in love can fully understand what it means.

So, what is the link between falling in love and the mental process you go through when you are suddenly transfixed by a concept, goal or idea?

Think back, but this time to a point in your career or personal life when you achieved a level of success. For example, a project that you had worked on for 12 months or more that finally came to fruition, was seen by others as successful and impressed your peers. Outside of work, perhaps you decided to learn a new language because you wanted to communicate better on holiday, or you wanted to take a course in how to coach your favourite sport to children in your spare time. Perhaps to your surprise, the task, once an interesting prospect, had become a passion.

Remember the feeling when you decided you were going to set out on a journey? You were thrilled, elated, overjoyed and, yes, something akin to being in love.

And even if it was not love at first sight, the passion was soon overwhelming. Perhaps the idea first presented itself as a problem that you were charged with solving – a process that, in itself, seemed less than appealing. However, once the initial feeling of being burdened had passed, you began to see the possibilities, not only for solving this problem, but also for what else the solution might enable you to achieve.

In other words, at some point, you recognised the task for what it really was – an adventure that would offer the potential for you to scale new heights and to achieve great success. And, for this to happen, it was almost inevitable that you fell in love with the idea.

Concept vs Process

That's not to say that you were in love with either the process or, indeed, the people around you; rather, you had fallen in love with the concept at its purest level and your passion drove you to ensure that the project was successful.

This is why the first steps on the road to achieving a new goal are not about setting specific targets. How could it be possible to set targets to fall in love? Certainly, you could put yourself in the best position to find another person by going to the right places, advertising yourself as available and presenting yourself in the best possible light – but does any of this ensure that you will fall in love? Of course not.

Another way of looking at how you first view an idea is to consider it in terms of appetite. When you realise you want to push for a promotion, to switch roles into an area that is more suited to your strengths or, indeed, decide that it's time you took on a new personal challenge, it is the size of your appetite for the task that will largely determine whether or not you will drive it forward.

Your aspirations are another key issue in determining your future. They have, at least in part, brought you to where you are now. You may not have recognised it at the time, and it may not have been a childhood dream, but doubtless you will have aspired to some aspect of your career – otherwise why choose that path? High aspirations + low achievement x zero appetite to improve = personal misery.

Dreams vs Reality

The late *Guardian* and *Independent* columnist Deborah Orr once wrote: 'There is a fine line between dreams and fantasies, and a great big distorting one between fantasy and reality.' (*Independent*, June 25, 2005)

While we have little or no influence over fantastical notions – such as winning the lottery – many of us harbour dreams that could come true if we could only get our act together, seize them and drag them out of the realm of dream and into the sphere of reality. They may be difficult and they may even be dangerous, but they are possible.

When I think back to the time I first heard about somebody rowing across the Atlantic in a small boat, I was intrigued by the idea and couldn't get it out of my mind. The same thing happened when I became aware of the challenge of the Marathon des Sables – running 156 miles across the Sahara in seven days. At the age of 60 and having not run a marathon for over 20 years, why on earth would I want to put myself through this gruelling endeavour that had a high risk of failure? Equally, why, with very little rowing experience, would I set off on a 3,000-mile voyage across the Atlantic that would take almost 10 weeks to complete?

If you were to ask 99 per cent of people if they'd commit to either the Marathon des Sables or rowing the Atlantic, they would probably say 'You must be mad.' And maybe they'd be right. Most people simply would not even consider taking on such potentially dangerous – and possibly ridiculous – challenges. But at those points in my life, I did care. I cared so much I had to do them.

The day-to-day struggles of life are more than enough for the great majority of people, but a sense of restlessness draws some to challenges that take them to the edge of their ability. Maybe the initial challenge is to try to work out what would give you that sense of passion and excitement. What is it that you really care about? And do you care about it enough to put yourself out on a limb to achieve it?

Critical questions to ask yourself:

- How would I define 'success' (for myself?)
- What do I really care about?
- What do I need to do to find the truly inspiring goal I am looking for?
- If I had an inspiring goal, what would it look/feel like?
- When am I at my most inspired?
- What are the challenges in my life that inspire me – right now?
- What do I need to achieve to be able to look back over my life and call it successful?

Chapter 2: CAPABLE

Have you got what it takes?

'If we did all the things we are capable of, we would literally astound ourselves'

— Thomas Edison, inventor

Capability – our power or ability to do something – is a deciding factor in the success or failure of any challenge or adventure we take on. Yet we are poor judges of our own capability, often underestimating what we can achieve. By better understanding our capability – our strengths and our weaknesses – we can set and achieve goals, in the world of business or adventure, that truly stretch and satisfy us.

Am I Capable?

Somebody once said to me that if you did not approach the formation of a new business with a spirit of innocence, you would never have the courage to even start. In other words, if you really knew the pain, hardship and stress that lay ahead, you would never embark on the journey. You would never begin your adventure.

So, I guess, one of the first major hurdles that faces us when we are drawn to something that feels challenging and adventurous is, 'Am I capable of doing it?'

The difficulty with this question, though, is that at this stage you don't have the answer; you don't know if you could succeed. To take the next step, you need to assess several factors.

Opportunity Costs

Opportunity costs are a serious consideration for an adventurer. What other opportunities/responsibilities/obligations should you turn away from to make space for the big one? What impact will this have on the rest of your life, and that of your family? Is it realistic and fair at this stage in your life?

Take it from me, these are uncomfortable questions to ask oneself and decisions based on the answers can seem unreasonable and unfair to loved ones.

But whether you are planning to scale an unclimbed peak, start your own business or get married, the question of capability is a crucial one. The choice you are about to make will have profound implications for you and those around you – particularly if the challenge is a serious one.

You must decide:
a) The challenge is worth the pain and discomfort, and,
b) That if you're not confident you have the capabilities now, you believe you can get them together before the implementation of your new project, idea or passion

Promotion Or Prevention?

In her book *Succeed: How We Can Reach Our Goals*,[1] social psychologist Heidi Grant Halvorson writes perceptively about setting goals. When it comes to goal-setting, she differentiates between those of us with a promotion focus and those with a prevention focus.

She describes the promotion focus as a move towards achievement and accomplishment – maximising gains and not missing opportunities. The prevention focus, by contrast, is more concerned with protecting ourselves from things going wrong. The emphasis is on safety and danger. We are also concerned about fulfilling our responsibilities. Our priority is minimising losses and trying to hang on to what we already have.

The example she gives in her book is that of the hunter in the wild who suddenly sees a flash of brown in the grass. In that instant, the hunter cannot be sure that the flash was an animal.

If the hunter is in a promotion-focused mindset, they will want to take a chance, to avoid losing the opportunity of a meal. Nothing ventured, nothing gained. They are said to have a 'risk bias' and tend to wind up with more food at the end of the day, but they also experience many more false alarms and waste a lot of ammunition. If the hunter is in a prevention-focused mindset, on the other hand, they are much more likely to play it safe and hold back. For them, it is important to make sure they see the animal before they shoot, rather than risk making a mistake. They hate false alarms. They have a 'conservative bias'. They won't scare away the animal unnecessarily or waste ammo but may come back empty-handed a little more often.

Both mindsets are valid. And most of us will use both at some point. But your default attitude towards risk will always have a huge impact on how you see your capability. When you start looking at a project such as rowing across an ocean, you cannot possibly know if you'll be capable of achieving that goal in 18 months' time, unless you're already an experienced and accomplished ocean rower. You can only imagine and hope this will become possible. Much capability can be developed – but only if you are prepared to take the risk and commit to developing the required proficiency in whatever time you have available before you set out. A big part of that commitment is to develop a promotion-focused mindset.

The good news is that your psychological profile regarding attitudes to risk can be measured. I regularly use these profiles when working with adventurers or adventurous business teams to find out if they are in the frame of mind for a serious challenge.

These online questionnaires measure your propensity for taking risks in various parts of your life: recreational, health and safety, social, financial and reputational. I continue to be fascinated by the very different approaches we have when faced with challenging situations.

So, in summary, until you can pass through this stage of capability, you will not be able to move forward with confidence to the next phase of your adventure. Unless you feel you have the capabilities, or you are sure you can develop them, you are setting yourself up for disappointment.

The Lure Of Uncertainty

Along with your capability to handle risk, you must also look at your capability to handle uncertainty. They are not the same thing. For example, I have met plenty of people who can cope with the risk of rock climbing on difficult, marked routes, but who would blanch at the thought of exploring unclimbed mountains in remote regions. The uncertainty would be too much for them. However, for me, one of the key defining characteristics of a true adventurer is the capability to set off on an endeavour – professional or personal – without knowing for sure what they might find.

This capability is highlighted for me in a book by Charles Blackmore, *Conquering the Desert of Death,*[2] in which he described his attempt to cross the Taklamakan Desert in northwest China with only a small team of men and some camels. Plenty of people before him had died trying to navigate this remote and dangerous part of the world. I heard Charles talking on a podcast recently and he said, in a throwaway remark, 'When doing expeditions, often you have to make decisions in the absence of facts.' For reasons beyond their control, he and his team were struggling at the start of the expedition to get their administration in place. In his book, he listed the logistical challenges they were facing, then noted: 'Should anything go wrong, I would justifiably be accused of incompetence or poor leadership. On the other hand, I knew from experience how important it was to get started and things would fall into place. There were bound to be many testing incidents which we couldn't hope to replicate in training.'

I think this sums up neatly the dilemma for the would-be adventurer. On the one hand, we have a moral responsibility to do everything we can to ensure our own safety and that of those we are leading. On the other hand, we must also develop our capability to not only live with uncertainty, but also to deliberately place ourselves in potentially uncertain situations.

The poet John Keats summed this up well in a letter in 1817, in which he described 'negative capability' – 'our ability to accept uncertainties, mysteries, doubts, without any irritable reaching after fact and reason'.

The 4 Stages Of Adventure

Rock climber and adventurer Colin Mortlock, who has spent a
lifetime engaging young people in outdoor adventure, wrote an
interesting and useful book, *The Adventure Alternative*,[3] in which
he identified four categories of adventure:

Stage One: Play

This is an activity that is fun while you are doing it. For some
adventurers, this would be considered a waste of time.

Stage Two: Adventure

This is an adventure situation (eg, rock climbing) where the
person feels in control and they are confident their experience
and abilities will ensure they can overcome any technical problem.
There is little or no fear of physical harm and there is a sense
of being in control. As Mortlock puts it, we feel 'comfortably
capable' in this phase.

Stage Three: Frontier Adventure

This kind of adventure often comes with some fear of physical
or psychological distress, and the adventurer no longer feels in
complete control of the situation. This is how Mortlock puts it:
'He feels, however, that he can, with considerable effort on his
part, and given luck, overcome the situation without accident.
If he succeeds, he has experienced what I would term "frontier
adventure". He has feelings of satisfaction, if not elation, about
the result.'

Stage Four: Misadventure

It is worth quoting Mortlock at length for this one: 'This is
the final stage – when the challenge is in any way beyond the
control of the person. In ultimate form, the result is death, but
between death and serious injuries on the one hand and frontier

adventure on the other, there are various degrees of both physical and psychological damage. In mild examples, the reaction will be one of immediate dissatisfaction and self-rebuke.'

It would be great if we could guarantee that our adventures remained in stage two or three. My experience suggests this is rarely the case. Instead, we are likely to go through several stages on a long adventure. There may well be times when stage two adventures unexpectedly swing into stage three. So the question for a potential adventurer is this: are you prepared to take on the risk of stage three or four adventures as part of the package? If the answer is 'yes', there are certain things you can do to increase your ability to handle challenging situations. I call these stretch experiences.

Stretch Experiences

Challenging, stressful and even frightening situations can help you build up a reservoir of resourcefulness and teach you how to adapt and react in a fast-changing environment. These punishing experiences may test you to your limits, but the benefits are considerable and can help you in many areas of your life.

Stretch experiences will be different for everyone: the important thing is that they push you beyond your comfort zone. Here are three types of stretch challenges: 1. Athletic; 2. Adventure; 3. Professional.

Athletic

Each type of endurance challenge will require its own kind of physical training. Some of the information you need can be picked up on the internet and from specialist magazines such as *Runner's World*. Some can be learnt from talking with others who have been there before you. (This is certainly the path I followed when rowing across the Atlantic and taking part in the Marathon des Sables.)

Some help can be gained from the support (paid or otherwise) of a professional sports coach. I have given a ton of free coaching support to people undertaking similar challenges to my own. It has always been my experience that people who have taken on endurance challenges are more than happy to share their experiences, which means any mistakes they made do not have to also become your mistakes. Their tips will be invaluable.

You will need to make sure your body is in top condition so you can put in your best physical performance. But do not overtrain. I have seen many people train too hard and end up having to pull out with injuries just before an event. Force yourself to train in conditions that will take you out of your comfort zone. Every time you make this stretch, you will build your resilience.

How do you train your mind to deal with the pain and monotony of an endurance event? The answer is by practising – over and over until your mind goes numb and you can switch off from the pain. I survived the Atlantic row and the desert challenge by perfecting a range of coping strategies. We will talk more about these later in the book.

Adventure

Much of the same advice applies here. However, the level of detail is more focused on the precise nature of the challenge. For example, if you are tackling a desert challenge, (a) you need to talk with people who have trodden the path before; (b) always take someone with you who has more experience than you do and can guide you, as well as save you hours of wasted time in research and planning; and (c) ideally, train in climates and conditions that are similar to those you will encounter on your adventure. So if you are heading for desert conditions, do hot-yoga sessions so your body becomes used to the extreme heat.

Practise taking yourself out of your comfort zone. I train on a series of muddy hills in the forest near where I live. When preparing for my North Pole challenge, I started dragging two heavy car tyres behind me to develop mental as well as physical resilience. When you are comfortable doing something like that, head out at night with a headtorch and get used to spooky birds suddenly flapping out in front of you. When you are comfortable with *that*, start loading up your rucksack. I take small groups of businesspeople to desert mountains in Africa twice a year and we regularly do two-hour training sessions on hilly forest trails with 25kg loads in our rucksacks. Throwing in a variety of challenges will help you to become more adaptable, which will be vital.

That said, as much as possible, your training needs to be specific to the terrain you will encounter: if you are going to be tackling a tough endurance challenge in a rugged mountainous region, or you are training for a mountain marathon, long sessions on flat tarmac will do little to prepare you – unless they are just a small part of your training schedule.

By the time you set foot on the terrain you have been preparing for, you ought to be feeling confident, capable and desperate to get cracking.

Professional

A typical situation is one in which people decide to leave their job and set up their own business. There is much to be learnt in making this transition and my advice is to start building your knowledge some time before you leave your job. If you are jumping from one lily pad to another, make sure the one you are landing on is solid enough to hold your weight. Before I left my job as a senior officer in the Metropolitan Police, I sought permission from my employer to do part-time business consultancy work in off-duty hours, to build up my skills, knowledge and experience. I went on a stack of courses; a few were paid for by my employers, as they were relevant to my role at the time, but I paid for many others. As often as you can, talk with others who are working in the field that interests you and seek their advice. Consider joining supportive professional organisations such as the Institute of Directors, to pick up current trends and gain access to free and paid-for professional advice.

Assess And Ask

Whatever the nature of your challenge, the key thing to work on is your capacity to handle uncertainty and risk. You have to learn how to change uncertainty into risk and know how to assess that risk. You also need to get used to changing anxiety into fear and keeping fear as your companion. We will discuss these concepts in detail in the Courage chapter.

Finally, when developing your capability, it is worth brainstorming with a coach to find out the skills, knowledge and abilities you will need to get you through the challenge. Then you need to do an audit of what is required to get up to speed and fix the deficit.

The Meniscus Zone

For the boundlessly optimistic, stretch experiences will be a natural part of life. We will stretch the boundaries of what we have been told is possible – sometimes to scary levels. If you watch water dripping from a tap into a glass, you will eventually see the level rise beyond the rim of the glass in a meniscus – a bubble of water that holds itself together above the glass with magic-like properties until, after one final drip, the bubble bursts and water runs down the glass. I have occasionally lived in this meniscus zone. Sometimes, it pays off and allows us into territory where quite extraordinary things can happen. Other times, alas, it does not.

Either way, when I think about capability, I also think about our capacity to make the stretch and to live in that meniscus zone – for it is here where some of the greatest adventures and experiences can be found.

Making It Real

The final area of capability I'd like to discuss has nothing to do with physical prowess or risk-taking, yet without it, there will be no adventure at all: the capability to turn an idea into a reality. I know a few people who would like to think of themselves as entrepreneurs, but their good ideas never quite come to life. They will tell you about their plans again and again, each time brimming with excitement and confidence, but they never put them into practice. If you want to do or experience extraordinary things and take on challenges outside your comfort zone, you also need the capability to make them happen.

It's not just about having bright ideas. Neither is it just about hard work. We'll look at this further in the Commit chapter. For now, when you think of your dream, you must be realistic about a few things:

(a) What your capacity is – in terms of your time and competing resources on a day-to-day basis.
(b) Whether you're prepared to put this plan at the top of your list of priorities right now.
(c) Whether you can manage the process yourself or need to outsource some of the work to other people who are more experienced and gifted in these areas.

Attitude to capacity is a stumbling block for people who are attempting the extraordinary. In fact, it often overshadows your capability to do something. I know plenty of senior businesspeople who are money-rich but time-poor. Time and again, they will reject offers of adventure because they cannot seem to find space for them in their diaries. So, my advice to would-be adventurers is to decide how much this challenge means to you. If you leave it until you have plenty of time, it will be like waiting for Godot – that time will never come. Anyone can find the capacity to take on challenges if they have sufficient motivation. But – and it is a big but – there will always be a trade-off somewhere. As my wise father-in-law often said, 'Life is an eternal compromise.'

Capability And The Golden Egg

Stephen Covey, author of *The 7 Habits of Highly Effective People*,[4] used the tale of *The Goose that Laid the Golden Eggs* to make a point that is relevant to my view on capability.

The Aesop fable tells the story of a poor farmer who one day discovers his goose has laid a golden egg. Better still, every morning thereafter the goose lays another golden egg. The farmer soon becomes extremely wealthy. But he also becomes greedy. So, in an attempt to get to all the remaining eggs at once, he kills and opens up the goose. Instead of finding lots of golden eggs, he finds nothing.

Covey says the moral of this fable is that true effectiveness is the function of two things: 1) what is produced (in this example, golden eggs); and 2) the producing asset or capacity to produce (the goose).

How does this affect the Seven Cs model? I see the golden eggs as the successful completion of a challenge. While the achievement itself should bring with it a sense of pride, true capability is not so much about coveting the golden eggs as it is about nurturing the goose that produces them.

So, instead of lurching from one adventure (or golden egg) to another, I challenge you to create in yourself a 'capability engine' that you can turn on and off as the situation demands. Arriving at this level of capability will stand you in good stead for a range of challenges, while avoiding the risk of burnout or becoming a one-trick pony.

Working with senior businesspeople, I've noticed that many have developed this capability engine. It enables them to be highly effective in their career and to take on great challenges outside of work – whether that's endurance events, charity work or just home improvement.

Achieving this kind of capability – which is more about the goose than the egg it produces – can enrich not only your life but also wider society. I read recently that the first cure for smallpox was discovered in the southwest of England in 1774.

A farmer, Benjamin Jesty, took some pus from the udders of a cowpox-infected cow and scratched it onto the skin of his (highly trusting) wife and sons. None of them contracted smallpox – but little was heard of the experiment at the time. Over 20 years later, a doctor from Gloucestershire, Edward Jenner, made similar observations and came to similar conclusions. It was he, not Jesty, who brought his findings to the public and was credited with inventing the lifesaving vaccine for smallpox. Jesty was interested in the golden egg; Jenner created the golden goose.

You must decide where your interest lies: 1) in reading about other people's golden eggs; 2) in creating a golden egg for yourself or; 3) creating a golden goose that will enrich not only your future but that of others. Whichever option you choose, you must be happy with the results. But if you want to truly expand your capability in a broader context, option 3 is the one to aim for.

The Locus Of Control

If you are going to be able to make sense of your capability and stretch it to extreme levels, you need to be able to work out what is within your locus of control and what is outside it.

The locus of control model was established in the 1950s by US psychologist Julian Rotter. The essence of this model is as simple as it is powerful. In life, we all experience joy and hardship. During the toughest moments, we may feel as though we're being tossed about on the sea of life. Our feelings of capability seem weak, and life feels unfair and out of our control. But during joyful moments, we feel excited by, and in charge of, our lives, masters of our own destinies and capable of tackling stretch tasks with ease and confidence.

Rotter defined the differences in these two attitudes in terms of a locus of control. When we're feeling down on our luck, complaining about our lot, we're expressing a belief in an *external* locus of control. By contrast, when we are feeling upbeat and on top of things, we're expressing a belief in an *internal* locus of control. So, what are the differences, and how do they influence the Seven Cs?

Internal locus of control

People with a strong internal locus of control believe they can influence the outcome of events. They take responsibility for their lives, their decisions and the events and circumstances that have led them to the situation in which they find themselves. They are not interested in concepts of 'luck' or 'fate', which others may feel predetermine outcomes; they typically feel that people create their own luck. If accidents or unhappy events take place, they consider what part they played in getting into the situation in the first place and feel they should shoulder the responsibility and find a solution. People with this mindset can get in touch with their capability and drive possibilities into uncharted areas of challenge.

External locus of control

People with an external locus of control are more likely to feel that life is preordained and that there is little they can do to influence things. They may believe that people are either lucky or unlucky in life, and that events are determined by fate. Their sense of their own capability is fragile and easily knocked down. Taken to extremes, the deeply embedded external locus of control can lead to a victim mentality or an attitude of learnt helplessness. Whether or not you have the courage to take risks and step into the unknown with a spirit of adventure will inevitably be influenced by your perception of your locus of control. Unsurprisingly, people with an internal locus of control will feel better about themselves, cope better with adversity and crises, and enjoy more success in life than those who have an external locus of control.

Using the Seven Cs model, and the questions at the end of each chapter, you'll be able to better understand your current locus of control and get a firmer grasp on your capability. Although we may choose the difficult and unpleasant circumstances in which we can find ourselves, we can, with practice, change our attitude to them. Establishing more of an internal locus of control is one very effective way of achieving this.

As for being lucky or unlucky, I subscribe to the view offered by the Roman philosopher Seneca, who said, 'Luck is what happens when preparation meets opportunity.'

Climbing The Matterhorn

In 1983 – when I was young – I decided to climb the Matterhorn (14,690ft) with some buddies. We were all in our late thirties and were fit, energetic, capable climbers. We engaged a couple of great British Mountain Guides, who trained us for a week in ice-climbing techniques and ensured we were capable of making an attempt on this notoriously dangerous mountain.

Having acclimatised to the altitude, polished up our skills and reached peak fitness, we were hovering – waiting for the bad weather to clear, waiting to take the chance to climb the mountain. If you have been to Zermatt, in Switzerland, you will know the power of the Matterhorn. Wherever you go, you look up and see it dominating the skyline and the valleys below.

Days ticked by and each morning we saw the mountain still bedecked in snow and ice, and therefore declared to be unclimbable. After 10 days, our window of opportunity closed and the rest of the team needed to return to work.

I was a chief inspector in the Metropolitan Police at the time and I explained to one of our guides, renowned climber Roger Baxter-Jones, that I had been asked by a teacher of deaf children if staff in the police station could raise more than £1,000 to pay for a radio hearing aid for one of her pupils. I told her I would raise the money, but had no idea how to do so (I was being promotion focused, perhaps). I decided to tackle the Matterhorn, having seen pictures and learnt what an awesome mountain it was.

Roger volunteered to guide me up the mountain, despite the challenging conditions, so we waited at advance base camp of the mountain for several days, hoping the weather would clear. But it didn't. Then I found out I was facing the sack if I did not return to work. When I told Roger this, he said, 'Look, we can do this tomorrow, shit or bust, but we may have to do it in winter conditions. I can't promise we will come back down alive.' I told him I'd rather die than return empty-handed. With that, we packed our kit for an early-morning climb the next day – whatever the conditions.

The epic climb is described in my first book, *Restless*, but suffice to say that we survived. The point is this: was I capable of climbing the Matterhorn under winter conditions at that stage in my life and coming down alive? In the moment I made the decision, I believed I *was* capable. And in my promotion-focused frame of mind, I made the right decision. In a prevention-focused mindset, I would have turned back – and missed the prize.

Critical questions to ask yourself:

- Do I have the knowledge, skills and abilities to achieve success as I define it? If not, how and when will I gain this knowledge?
- Am I comfortable living with uncertainty for extended periods?
- Have I seriously researched the risks involved?
- Do I have the mental capacity to handle the risk?
- Thinking about the levels of adventure, at what level am I prepared to operate?
- Is my goal achievable?
- What is my capacity – in terms of time and competing resources?
- Am I prepared to put this at the top of the list of priorities in my life?
- Can I manage the entrepreneurial process myself, or do I need to outsource some of the work to other people?
- Can I afford to be away from work for the number of days required?
- Can I get approval from my wife/husband/partner to be away for the number of days required?
- Am I prepared to put loved ones through a level of worry and anxiety around my personal safety?

Chapter 3: CURIOSITY

Do you know how to find out what you need?

'You see things and you say, "Why?"
But I dream things that never were, and I say, "Why not?"

– George Bernard Shaw, playwright

Curiosity is the secret additive to the fuel that gives the Seven Cs' engine its power. Without it, our lives remain in a steady (what I call 'transactional') state. If you are to find fresh ways to conquer challenges that are at the edge of your capability, you need this additive in your daily diet – just as long-distance mountain runners need energy gels to help them go the distance. If you want to be an adventurer, you must develop a sense of curiosity. You will be amazed how it turbocharges your progress to an exciting future.

The Curious Brain

When I am coaching clients, individually or in teams, some of my focus is on helping them understand how their personality type or preferred way of thinking affects their decision-making and, ultimately, their effectiveness in a range of business scenarios.

Neuroscience has given us a clear picture of the ways the left side and right side of the brain influence our personality and how we approach life. You are said to be left-brained if your thinking approach is mostly analytical, methodical and objective. If your natural approach tends to be more creative, intuitive and thoughtful, you are said to be right-brained.

You might conclude that people who are right-brain dominant are more likely to have a better developed sense of curiosity than those with a left-brain dominance. But my experience of working with all kinds of personality types tells me this is not the case.

Indeed, one of the most analytical men in history was also one of the most curious: Albert Einstein. That curiosity is encapsulated in one of my favourite quotes of his: 'Most people stop looking when they find the proverbial needle in the haystack. I would continue looking to see if there were other needles.'

One of the things that made Einstein so remarkable was his ability to harness the creative and analytical sides of his brain to equal effect. And the same applies to other geniuses, such as Leonardo da Vinci, whose achievements are as diverse as they are extraordinary.

What does this mean in practice? I believe it suggests that curiosity is a product of both sides of the brain. So you must find ways of allowing your brain to range way beyond your natural way of thinking – thinking outside the box, if you like – and at the same time be prepared to go into ruthless analytical research about the challenge you plan to face.

Adventurers As 'Curious Explorers'

In his book, *Curious?*,[1] psychologist and wellbeing expert Todd Kashdan offers a neat summation of the topic: 'Living a life of curiosity is not about ignoring risk and anxiety. It's about being willing to do what one values, even in the face of risk and anxiety.'

Kashdan writes about what he calls 'curious explorers', describing them as people who are comfortable with the risk of taking on challenges and have a 'lust for the new'. He is particularly insightful about the potential crossover benefits of cultivating curiosity:

'When we are probing the nooks and crannies of new worlds,' he writes, 'inevitably we are also learning. This is the ultimate goal of our curiosity system: to add to our existing knowledge, skills and competencies. These additions help us to better understand ourselves and the outside world, cope with challenges of everyday life and improve our ability to handle chaos.'

The Surprising Benefits Of Curiosity

When I look back on my life – at the age of 76 – I find that some of my more unusual – but still exciting – achievements have been in the world of home-building or DIY.

One that sticks in my mind happened about 40 years ago when I was working as a police inspector. I remember sitting in the police canteen one night, chatting with a colleague who had just employed a plumbing firm to install central heating in his house. I told him my family and I had recently moved into a small terraced house and would love to have central heating, but it would be quite a while before we could afford it. He said, 'Why don't you do it yourself?'

The idea of installing a new plumbing system – with no experience, training or qualification – was daunting. But it did have a certain allure. It seemed an impossible idea, but breaking through impossibility has always excited me.

I asked my colleague, 'How would I even start?' His advice was to go to a library and get a DIY book about plumbing. He explained that the cost of plumbing tools and pipes did not form a big part of the total expense. The bulk of the cost, quite reasonably, was for the supply of skilled labour.

The challenge was tantalising. First, I found the perfect book that explained in detail how to calculate the size of radiators for each room and how to weld pipes together.

Then I found a place that would sell me plumbing equipment at heavily discounted prices. I started experimenting and learning how to weld pipes. I hung my first radiator on the wall. I learnt how to take up floorboards and to lay down pipes with insulation around them. Over time, I inched my way through the house and, before I knew it, I had installed a new heating system.

It would be wrong to underplay the serious and stressful nature of this project. I had a young family at the time and a new puppy that kept running under the floorboards. It took me far more time than a plumber would've needed and the results were probably a lot less professional. But we achieved a goal in a few months that would've taken several years if we had waited until we'd saved enough money.

So, when I analyse this case study, what are the elements that seem important in relation to curiosity?

1. The moment a challenge comes, your curiosity should be aroused. You should be instantly thinking – is this one for me?

2. You need to constantly have your antennae scanning for new ideas, new possibilities, new ways of learning.

3. You should be curious about things even if they don't seem immediately relevant to your situation – tuck the information in the back of your brain to draw on when needed.

4. When talking to professionals in one field, don't be afraid to ask them for information or recommendations about allied fields.

5. Value and respect trusted professionals. But work out what you can do yourself wherever you can. That way, you push the boundaries of possibilities for yourself throughout your life.

6. Remember: there is nothing wrong with exploring possibilities or experimenting (Thomas Edison and his team are reputed to have tested more than 3,000 designs and theories before coming up with a workable lightbulb). Don't be afraid of trial and error as you take baby steps towards your big goal. You can always back out if it becomes clear you do not have the capability required to achieve your goal.

If there are DIY challenges in my house or I have a problem with the car, instead of dreading dealing with them, I feel quite excited and wonder if I can tackle them myself. I am no more capable than the next person and I am certainly no mechanical genius; however, I do have a strong desire to take on challenges that might, to others, seem insurmountable. My advice to you is to develop that same hunger for challenge, together with the capability of living in a space of uncertainty and potential risk without losing that feeling of excitement and hope.

Growth vs Fixed Mindset

Curiosity is a crucial ingredient that underpins what is described as a 'growth mindset'. The idea was developed by the psychologist

Carol Dweck. In essence, it comes down to how you view yourself. Do you believe your talents and abilities are fixed, or do you believe you can improve through effort and focused practice? When you experience a setback, do you tell yourself you're rubbish and retreat into your comfort zone? Or do you look at it as a learning experience? With a growth mindset, rather than a fixed one, you embrace the possibility of failure – and you maintain a curiosity about future challenges. As Dweck writes: 'The passion for stretching yourself and sticking to it, even (or especially) when it's not going well, is the hallmark of the growth mindset. This is the mindset that allows people to thrive during some of the most challenging times in their lives.'[2]

Curiosity In Business

A few years ago, I ran a conference in London for some blue-chip companies, including major banks. The purpose of the event was to examine the characteristics of potential high-flyers with a view to learning how they could be managed more effectively.

Before the conference, we researched the tendencies of high-flyers whose careers had been derailed. Interestingly, one of the traits that divided those who had stalled from those who had continued their rise towards success was that they had, almost without exception, failed to learn from the fires of their experience.

It is entirely justifiable (and, in many ways, helpful) for people to make mistakes and experience periods of confusion and chaos when engaged in hazardous pursuits. If you are to have the confidence to allow your curiosity free rein, you must accept – and expect – the occasional mistake.

As business leaders, it is vital that we encourage those we lead to exercise their curiosity without fear of unfair repercussions if their judgments and guesses don't always hit the mark.

It is easy – and forgivable – to make mistakes. It is only unwise to repeat those mistakes and fail to learn from them.

Curiosity And Energy

Curiosity and energy are inextricably connected. As Todd Kashdan writes in *Curious?*: 'We need energy to act on our curiosity, and we need curiosity to discover what works to replenish our energy.'

This chimes with my own experience. At times, when I've been overworking and am feeling anxious, my curiosity drive is low. And having given free coaching sessions to people whose businesses crashed because of the coronavirus pandemic, I've noticed something: people whose levels of curiosity would normally be high were unable to see the simple steps that could help them break out of their situations.

Very often, the rekindling of a person's curiosity can spark one idea that will send them away with a fresh sense of hope. So, the questions for all of us are: what does it take to spark our curiosity? And where, when and how can we find the creative space to work out the solutions to problems that stand in the way of our success?

Curiosity And 'The Buttons Of Opportunity'

Carlos Castaneda, in his book *Journey to Ixtlan*, talks about 'the buttons of opportunity' available to all of us.

'All of us, whether or not we are warriors, have a cubic centimetre of chance that pops out in front of our eyes from time to time. The difference between an average man and a warrior is that the warrior is aware of this, and one of his tasks is to be alert, deliberately waiting, so that when his cubic centimetre pops out he has the necessary speed, the power to pick it up.'[3]

The buttons of opportunity are there for all of us, if only we can spot them. The difficulty is that we fill our lives with so much clutter.

The Conveyor Belt Of Life

I sometimes recall the TV programme *The Generation Game*, with Bruce Forsyth. Those of you who are old enough will remember that at a key point in the show, contestants would sit in front of a conveyer belt as prizes passed by. The challenge for them was to try to hold in their mind all the prizes and to recall as many as possible in the show's finale. Whatever they could remember, they could keep.

I imagine a young guy winning a load of prizes, taking them home to his partner, announcing what he'd won ('A toaster! A cuddly toy!') and being informed, much to his disappointment, that they neither needed nor wanted any of these items.

So it is when we surround ourselves with the winnings of the conveyor belt of life. We stumble from one ridiculous purchase to the next, convincing ourselves that, somehow, they will make us happy. In reality, they simply clutter up our life. There is no chance we will spot our own critical 'buttons of opportunity' if we are constantly smothering them with unnecessary clutter.

The secret of success for anyone looking to take on a transformational challenge is to work out what opportunities you need to bring your dream into reality. You then need to be poised – ready to grab those buttons for yourself.

Ascents Of Curiosity

Some of the happiest (and, at times, scariest) moments of my early life came in the late 1960s, when I was learning the art of rock climbing with my cousin. We were both 18. Nowadays, climbers are equipped with sophisticated gear to attach themselves to the rock face, as well as specialist climbing shoes. None of that was available to us. If you fell, you were looking at a long drop and little chance of survival.

Also, in those early days, many of the routes in climbing guidebooks were described in a language that did not make a lot of sense (unless you were an experienced climber). So, you set off with one six-foot sling of tape and the hope that somehow you would find a way to the summit. It was eternal curiosity – and not a little hope – that led you on to the next pitch.

You don't need to cultivate your curiosity on a sheer rock face. The opportunities to explore and expand your boundaries can be found in myriad places – from the mountains to the boardroom. And the benefits of doing so can be felt personally and professionally.

Critical questions to ask yourself:

- Is my craving for certainty hindering opportunities for my curiosity to flourish?
- Do I have a growth or a fixed mindset?
- When and where do I find moments of fizz, when my curiosity is free to run unchained?
- What am I curious about?
- What distractions piling up on the conveyor belt of life are standing in the way of my success?
- Can I identify the buttons of opportunity I have seized in life so far? What about those I've missed?
- How much opportunity have I given for my curiosity to flourish?
- Make a list of the people I know or have met who have an amazingly productive curiosity

Chapter 4: COMMIT

Are you ready to go all in?

'Commitment is doing what you said you would, long after the mood in which you said it has left'

– George Zalucki, psychologist and personal-growth guru

Imagine the moment when two trapeze artists head towards each other. They know that at a crucial point they must both let go and fly through the air to catch their partner's trapeze. They loosen their grip and they are airborne. This is the point of no return – the true moment of commitment. In this chapter, we'll discuss the meaning of that word, what stops people from committing and how you can master the art of commitment.

What Is Commitment?

Dictionary definitions of 'commitment' don't seem to do justice to the power I see behind the word. They describe 'an agreement or pledge to do something', or a 'promise to do something in the future'. This has a passionless, contractual feel to it. For me, the word 'commit' pulsates with energy: I am not talking about a promise to do something, sometime, or an agreement to carry out a task for someone else. No, I am talking about a commitment to yourself to do something right on the edge of your capability.

Why Is It Important?

The issue of commitment infuses every section of the Seven Cs model. It is commitment that gets you to the starting line. It is also what will drive you forward when everything in your head is screaming 'Stop!'. It means you would rather die in the process than give up through lack of effort.

The good news is that once you make the decision, nothing inside you will stop you achieving success. Yes, there will be objective risks that can pop up to challenge you. Some of these may be insurmountable. But you will never fail through lack of effort. If you are driven back by external forces beyond your control, you can hold your head up high and know you have given it your all. Retreat can then be an honourable decision.

There is always another day. What you do not want, though, are the sleepless nights that follow a failure to commit.

So, my advice is to look seriously at the depth of your commitment. On a scale of one to ten, if you are not able to give it seven or above, the time is not right for you to go ahead.

What Does It Feel Like To Commit?

If the Care stage in the model is all about falling in love with an idea, the Commit stage is about getting married to an idea.

Indeed, making this commitment shares a similarity with the moment someone proposes and the other person accepts. There may or may not be any sense of rationality about the decision. There will probably have been plenty of hovering before this point, but there is a sudden moment of potency when you know for certain you are moving forward. Now it is inevitable.

So, as you begin preparing for the challenge ahead, it might be wise to ask yourself whether you have reached a point of true commitment, or if you are still on the pathway of curiosity, or wrestling with doubts about your capability.

For me, every time I have reached this critical point on my journey towards adventure, I can sense something of a lightbulb moment of commitment, beyond which there is no turning back. It's scary, but also hugely empowering.

Whether you are setting yourself up to tackle your first physical endurance challenge, buying your first house or flat, or deciding to start a family, there will come a decision that marks the moment of commitment, after which all sorts of doors will start to open for you. But until you reach this stage, your dream will remain out of reach.

Stand Up And Be Counted

To commit to an adventure, you must be prepared to stand up with genuine confidence and take responsibility for what you are about to do. You have to stand up and be counted in the face of criticism from others. You also have to face yourself.

If you are involving other people, and you are in a leadership role, you need to tell them where you are going and how you are going to get there. There must be no ifs or buts at this stage.

If you have made that jump into commitment with genuine belief and total engagement, people will see it in your eyes. If they know you and trust you, they will follow you through to the end.

What Will You Sacrifice?

In his 1984 book, *Death in the Locker Room*,[1] Dr Bob Goldman posed a powerful, provocative question to 198 athletes:

'If I had a magic drug that was so fantastic that if you took it once you would win every competition you would enter, from the Olympic Decathlon to Mr Universe, for the next five years, but it had one minor drawback – it would kill you five years after you took it – would you still take the drug?'

Approximately half the athletes said they would take the drug regardless of what lay ahead. Subsequent experiments found far lower numbers willing to take the drug, but, for me, this survey remains a great example of the ultimate commitment to care.

While most of us aren't faced with such stark ultimatums, embarking on a challenge, particularly one with attendant dangers, does test our commitment. Self-help author Napoleon Hill wrote engagingly about this subject.[2] He recognised the pathway from the initial 'desire', (what we are calling Care in our model) as a period of restless energy until the vision starts coming together. Then came the inevitable challenge that appeared to block your path. He wrote that this was necessary, as it would harden your resolve. Only then would you realise how important this mission was for you.

Challenges can come in many forms: an injury in the build-up to an event, someone doubting your ability to succeed, a potential team member dropping out. But sometimes the biggest challenges come from the people who love you. It can be heartbreaking to turn away from their advice or commit to being away from family and friends for an extended period. Not all adventures are worth that price, but if you are to go forward you must make peace with your decision and fully commit to what lies ahead. To commit, you need courage (which we'll explore in a later chapter). For now, let me say that the hardest part is making that first move. On my adventures, courage was not difficult to come by when I was most in danger. The time when I really needed the courage was in truly committing to the challenge. The moment we do that, things begin to fall into place. Once we have the courage to commit, we will have the courage to complete.

One of the fascinating aspects of my work with high-performance teams is seeing individuals grappling with the two different approaches that feel embedded in their colleagues' personalities – promotion focus versus prevention focus (discussed in detail in the Capable chapter). Both have value, but the challenge for us as adventurers is that if our prevention focus is very strong, it may stop us from getting across the starting line when uncertainty and lack of clarity abound. Equally, the challenge for us if we have a naturally high promotion focus is that we may well get across the starting line but fall at the first hurdle.

How Can You Learn To Commit?

I love the lecture 'Sliding Vs Deciding'[3] that was given by relationship expert Dr Scott Stanley. In it, he talks in detail about the difference between:
(a) drifting into a marriage after a period of cohabitation (where the final decision to marry has sometimes been triggered by pregnancy or a financial convenience). This he calls 'sliding';
    and
(b) making a decision to marry someone. His research suggests that couples who decide to get married statistically have a much better chance of a long-term union than those who drift or slide into their marriage.

The same principles apply to many decisions in life. If you're going to take on a challenge that has serious ramifications for you and others, it is vital that you decide to go forward with utter commitment and determination. From my experience, nothing less will bring success.

Building Resilience

It is easier to fully commit to something when you have primed both your body and mind. In other words, you need to build the physical and mental resilience relevant to your challenge.

This means getting out there and trying to recreate some of the situations you are likely to face on your adventure.

If you are looking at doing a chilly challenge such as a winter triathlon, you'd be wise to spend two minutes in a cold shower every day (a prospect that terrifies me, as I hate cold water).

If you are planning a mountain marathon, you need to train on rough ground in bad weather conditions. When you look out of your window and see that it is sheeting down with rain, that's the time to head out, instead of saying, 'I'll leave my training session until later.'

We will talk more about resilience in the final chapter, Courage, but I cannot urge you strongly enough to get out in tough conditions and put yourself under pressure. Not only are you training your body to take the knocks, but you are also training your mind to be resilient in a way that will enable you to persevere during the toughest moments of your adventure or challenge.

Sharing A Goal With Others

Does sharing your goals with others help you to commit? Yes and no.

You might assume that sharing your goal with someone would help to hold you accountable to making that goal a success. However, it's critical you consider carefully who you are allowing yourself to be accountable to and to think about what that accountability should look like.

Studies show that your accountability buddy should be a friend. Strangely enough, when your progress is being monitored by a stranger, it can have a demotivating effect. Research has also demonstrated that the person you share your goals with should have some level of skill in supporting you; this could take the form of their experience as a coach or expertise in the area of your endeavour. Their feedback should be based on your effort and what you've achieved, rather than your ability. In technical terms, according to a study from Columbia University, that person should give you 'process' praise rather than 'person' praise.[4]

Another piece of research, published in the *Journal of Applied Psychology*,[5] suggests there are particular benefits to sharing your goals with a person you judge to be of higher status than you. This could be a family member, a close friend, a colleague, a mentor, a coach or a personal adviser. Sharing with such a person not only increases your accountability, but also will help you clarify some aspects of your goal.

Write Down Your Goals

Whether or not you share your goals with other people, one thing that does seem crucial when trying to enhance your commitment to setting goals is to write them down. A 2015 study[6] on goal strategies found that 70 per cent of participants who sent weekly updates to a friend either achieved or were well on the way to achieving their goals, compared with 35 per cent who kept their progress to themselves.

From my own experience, setting goals has been pivotal to my success in achieving extraordinary things. I have also witnessed huge leaps of success in people I coach who set themselves goals, write them down and review them regularly.

Skin In The Game

Over the past 20 years or so, I have consulted to many management buyout teams and start-up companies who have relied on investment from venture capitalists. The directors of the new businesses had often had to put a chunk of their house into the financial mix. This could have been avoided in some cases, but the venture capitalists wanted to see that the directors were truly committed to the venture. The term they often used was having 'skin in the game'. I think that concept is particularly relevant to the topic of commitment.

I was once asked to meet someone – in an advisory mentor role – who was putting together a team to trek to the North Pole. The guy was clearly excited about the project, so he scored highly on the care element. He had also done quite a bit of research. And although he appeared to have had little experience of endurance events, there was no reason why he could not have become fit enough to take on this challenge. However, when I asked him how he would finance this charity fundraising endeavour (which was going to cost in the region of £100,000), he told me he was hoping to raise money from sponsorship.

As I left the meeting, I sensed this guy would never achieve his objective. After some contemplation, I spoke with the person who had introduced me to him and asked if I should say what I felt. I was encouraged to go ahead, so I wrote an email to the prospective adventurer and told him of my concerns. Having had a lot of experience of trying to get sponsorship for expeditions, and having met many others who had tried the same thing, I was dubious about his chances of success. Unless he was prepared to fund the event himself, my belief was the expedition was doomed to failure. I never heard from that adventurer again.

Don't get me wrong: it is always great to have a crack at raising sponsorship for an expedition. But in my view, unless you are prepared to underwrite the challenge yourself, you are failing to truly commit to the event.

Oar Or Nothing

I learnt a good deal about commitment during my row across the Atlantic Ocean. This kind of adventure leaves no room for doubt or the possibility of failure – you truly have to burn your bridges behind you. Such is the power of the Atlantic's 30-foot waves that there is just no way to turn a boat around. The only way is forward.

My rowing partner and I realised fairly soon after setting off from La Gomera, one of the smallest of the Canary Islands, that it was going to be an awesome undertaking. We had no concept of the nature of the storms we'd be rowing in or the size of the waves we'd encounter.

It became clear that the only chance we had of completing the crossing was to keep the boat moving as fast as we could. To do this, we would need to row for two hours and rest for two hours, day and night, until the end of the adventure.

Imagine going to your local gym, sitting on a rowing machine and rowing for two hours, then trying to sleep for two hours, then starting again. Then imagine doing that for nearly 10 weeks with never a day off. Some days we were scorched by the sun – temperatures often exceeded 40°C – and some days we were lashed by wind and chilling rain or pounded by huge waves in the depths of the night. This was the reality of the commitment we had made. It was the power of that commitment that would keep us on course and bring us to our destination in Barbados, 3,000 miles from where we'd started.

Critical questions to ask yourself:

- Think of a time when I was totally committed to something – what did it feel like?
- What does it take to get my true commitment?
- What can detract from my commitment?
- What price would I have to pay for success, as I define it?
- Am I prepared to pay that price?
- Who can I share my goals with?
- Have I written down my goals?
- Do I have enough skin in the game?
- What are the gremlins that damage my confidence and hold me back from achieving my true potential?

Chapter 5: CLARITY

Are you clear about your goal?

'People do not wander around and then find themselves at the top of Mount Everest'

– Zig Ziglar, motivational speaker

When it comes to any adventure, there is a 'how' and there is a 'why'. At this stage, you should have worked out that you care deeply about this adventure. You should also have investigated and tapped into your curiosity, and researched supportive information. You should be sure you are capable of succeeding and have figured out how to free up capacity in your life to give this your all. And you should have mentally activated the 'engage' lever and committed to the adventure 100 per cent. This is all part of *how* you put a plan into action; but it can fall apart unless you clearly understand *why* you're doing it. That's what this chapter is about.

Restless

When I was planning to row across the Atlantic, friends would often ask, 'But *why* are you doing it?' It was a fair question. The voyage was clearly dangerous, would take several months and I was nearly 60 years of age. Why *did* I want to do it?

I knew I should have had an answer for them. But I didn't. What I had, instead, was a deep, burning desire to attack the challenge and somehow find a way to the other side – hopefully in one piece.

With the wisdom of hindsight, I can look back and see exactly why I did it. I wish these reasons were more noble and honorable, but the truth is, I had (not for the first time) arrived at a low ebb. My business was successful but the work was becoming tedious. My relationship with my business partner was in decline for several reasons – many of them my fault. I had a feeling that my life was not going anywhere. I needed a boost, a serious challenge. I was, as the title of that first book suggests, restless.

How could I carry on with enthusiasm in my work – which was all about coaching leaders and teams in a way that was inspirational and transformational – when I felt I was losing that cutting edge myself?

I understood the theory of 'stretch' assignments that would throw a person into the crucible of life in such a way that they would come back different and – hopefully – stronger. So why didn't I put it to the test myself?

Had I understood my reasons at the time, the journey across the Atlantic would have been more purposeful than it actually was. A driving motivation would have been a great help in my worst moments in the dark heart of the ocean.

So, as you enter this next stage of your preparation, I urge you to find the real purpose of your adventure. It will be time well spent, as it can steel you for the challenge ahead. As Friedrich Nietzsche wrote, 'He who has a why to live for can bear almost any how.'

Working To Understand 'Why'

When you're in the early stages of an adventure, the last thing you want to do is justify why you are so intoxicated with an idea, dream or ambition. To try to articulate your true purpose at this point would be either impossible or incredibly dull. The whole point of this early stage is that you are stoking up the fires of energy and excitement for the adventure. It may be, though, that the true fire has not yet been lit.

As the planning stage advances, however, it pays to analyse what it is about the adventure that you find so intoxicating. If you had met somebody, fallen in love with them, decided to commit to spending the rest of your life with them and sealed your relationship, a good friend might reasonably ask, 'What is it about this person that makes you so certain?' You answer might be a simple one: 'I can't live without them' or 'All I know is that I want to spend the rest of my life with them.'

And it might be that the key initial attraction was your partner's stunning good looks, sexuality, intelligence, sense of humour, shared interests and so on.

So it is with an adventure. You must try to be honest with yourself and define what it is that makes you certain you want to commit to it and see it through to the end.

Appetites wax and wane. The intoxicating power of that early stage of falling in love cannot last forever. Therefore, it is wise to conduct a quick review of how you are feeling about your challenge at this stage.

Where you are right now:

1. Is your decision rational or emotional?
2. What is driving you?
3. How do you feel about your capability at this stage?
4. Have you allowed your curiosity free rein to explore every avenue to ensure you can make progress?
5. Have you plucked up the courage to speak to others who are likely to be affected by your decision?
6. Are you running towards this adventure or running away from something else?
7. If someone asked you why are you doing this, how would you answer?

Talent vs Skills

Let us assume, then, that you have spent some time alone and can now explain your reasons for doing what you are doing. Now you must be clear about what the path to success looks like.

This is about (a) tying goals down to a process of delivery; (b) focusing on the right goals and dispensing with the wrong ones; and (c) being committed to making them happen.

Psychologist Angela Duckworth has some interesting things to say about bringing an adventure to life. In her book *GRIT: Why Passion and Resilience are the Secrets to Success*,[1] she starts by trying to understand what part talent plays in success. Duckworth believes that talent alone is not enough: many of us have the natural ability to do something but may be unaware of this potential. Talent only comes alive when:

1. We recognise it or value it, and

2. We realise we need it and are prepared, if necessary, to put significant effort into developing it.

Duckworth believes effort, not talent, is the secret to success: 'Without effort, your talent is nothing more than your unmet potential. Without effort, your skill is nothing more than what you could have done but didn't. With effort, talent becomes skill and at the very same time, effort makes skill productive.'

At this stage, then, I think it's incumbent on any aspiring adventurer to look at the talent and skills they have – and think about the effort it will take to develop them.

This is when you focus intently on your capability. In the Capability chapter, I said it was not critical at that stage that you knew precisely your level of capability in relation to your challenge. But you did need to understand what your capability would *need to be* at a later stage, when you would face the challenge.

Now that you are committed to the event, you need to be brutally honest about your present level of capability and the level you must attain to move forward.

It is time to do an audit of your skill levels. And you should also ratchet up your level of connection with people who have faced your challenge before. We will talk more about this in the next chapter, Connect.

For me, this is also the time when you need to develop your ability to stretch beyond your comfort zone. It is time to take the boat out of the safety of the estuary, put up the sails and set out to sea.

When you're taking on a project that challenges your strength and endurance, or one that is going to demand considerable depths of courage, you have to develop your capability – not only in terms of physical strength, but also in terms of your capability to withstand prolonged periods of pain and discomfort. If it is a climbing challenge, start pushing yourself up rock faces that will bring you to the edge of your comfort zone. If it is a sea-based challenge, head for choppy waters and face harsh weather. If it is a new business challenge, start thinking about what your realistic capacity (time and resources) is now and what it will need to be. What exactly are you prepared to risk?

Scenario Planning

At this stage, it's also useful to brainstorm the range of things that could challenge your success, or, indeed, your life, when you embark on your adventure. Only then can you say you are ready for anything that fate can throw at you.

Clearly, there's always the potential to be blindsided by something. But your job as an adventurer is simply to predict as much as you can and then be able to brace yourself for the worst life can throw at you. To do this, you must hone your capability to live with whatever comes your way.

Becoming Utterly Focused

To achieve clarity, you must have focus. The early will and desire for the adventure must now be accompanied by rational thinking. Falling in love with an idea is not the same as maturing a focused vision. It is the vision that will ultimately get you there; the idea just keeps you awake at night.

When I think of being utterly focused, I think of the determination I see in a young guy I know who is committed to setting up a self-sustaining business in Uganda to help orphans who have Aids. His drive comes from the belief he can do something to help the lives of others – as opposed to helping large corporations make money, as he had done previously. He has found the 'why', the clarity of purpose that will sustain him for the next 30 years.

In my experience, the universe has a strange way of working in your favour when you find that clarity. I'm reminded of a quote attributed to the great German writer Goethe: 'The moment one definitely commits oneself, then providence moves, too.' Many a time, when I have pushed the lever to commit and burned bridges behind me, a benefactor has come out of nowhere to save my bacon. It felt like fate (or providence) paying me back for my faith and trust. It's hard to say why, but there's one thing I know for sure: when you have a clarity of purpose, people are drawn to you and good things happen.

Seeking Clarity

In my experience, people with clarity have four things in common:
1. A definite purpose backed by a burning desire to fulfil it
2. A definite plan, expressed in continuous action
3. A mind closed tightly against all negative suggestions from relatives, friends and acquaintances
4. A friendly alliance with one or more people who will encourage them to follow through with both plan and purpose

Goal Clarity And Goal Conflict

To achieve clarity, it is necessary to strip away the noise and clutter to focus on the few things that are truly important. In *GRIT*, Duckworth describes it as follows: 'What I mean is that you care about that *same* ultimate goal in an abiding, loyal, steady way. You are not capricious. Each day, you wake up thinking about the questions you fell asleep thinking about.

'At the extreme, one might call your focus obsessive. Most of your actions derive their significance from their allegiance to your ultimate concern, your life philosophy. You have your priorities in order ... It is about holding the same top-level goal for a very long time'.

For Duckworth, the crucial thing is to focus on one unifying goal, and once you know what that is, you can avoid goal conflict. In her words: 'You need one internal compass – not two, three, four or five.'

It's OK to have a hierarchy of supporting goals beneath this – as long as they support your top-level goal and are not a distraction from it or in conflict with it. You can change the supporting goals at any time, but the higher level goal is written in indelible ink. That goal will hold you on course and help you to succeed. This thinking can be illustrated through a goal pyramid.

Goal Pyramid Model

Primary goal

This model is well known in coaching. It is vital to keep your primary goal in mind. You'd be surprised how easy it is to lose sight of what you are trying to achieve when you are stuck under a mountain of admin. It is a matter of holding focus when, at times, it will feel like you are shooting at a moving target – or one you cannot even see.

Intermediate goals

There will be some key milestones that are crucial to your success – you need to know what they are and when they need to be achieved. Using the ocean-rowing example, a list of a few key milestone would be:

1. Where will your boat come from?
2. Where will your funding come from?
3. Are you going solo or with someone else?
4. How are you going to learn to row properly?
5. How are you going to learn how to navigate?

Short-term goals

From my experience, there is a never-ending list of admin jobs that will inch you closer to your intermediate goals. It's wise to have a good planning system to keep track of these tasks and do everything you can to tick them off each day. If you get to the end of the day and you have not made that call or completed that spreadsheet, you are not moving forward. This is not always easy – particularly if you have a busy day job and a family/partner to consider.

Some examples for an expedition leader could be:
1. Team selection
2. Regular briefings for team members
3. Kit and rations – how much for how many people and for how many days
4. Visas and entry requirements, and liaison with local authorities
5. Calls to potential sponsors
6. Map and journal research
7. Personal-fitness training schedule

How Much Will It Cost?

The one element that I typically neglect – though it's probably the most important one – is cost.

Anyone who has been involved in building projects will know that people tend to grossly underestimate costs. Typically, we end up over budget. This is the same with adventure projects and starting up small businesses.

It can be a deeply dispiriting moment when you reach an advanced point in your planning and realise that your numbers do not add up. But don't lose heart. If the figure is proving higher than you'd imagined, you can press on regardless, hoping you'll be able to somehow raise the money. But it's better to do this with your eyes open, rather than being shocked by the final cost further down the line. You must be honest with yourself about money.

When Clarity Pays Off

The row across the Atlantic taught me a lesson about the importance of a clarity of purpose. So, two years later, when I decided to enter the Marathon des Sables, my two goals were crystal clear:

1. At 60 years of age, I was never going to be able to play a competitive role in the race. So, my goal was simply to get through each day of the event in one piece, without being disqualified.
2. Having been told that participants would not be permitted to go swimming in the hotel pool when we finally finished (because we'd all have infected blisters on our feet), I would do whatever it took to avoid blisters, thereby remaining eligible for a post-race dip.

It was a joy to achieve these goals. They kept me engaged and focused throughout the event. And I cannot tell you how good it felt to plunge into the refreshing water of that swimming pool while the other finishers lay on sun loungers, unable to swim because of their blisters.

Critical questions to ask yourself:

- What is it about this challenge that I find so alluring?
- Why must I do it right now?
- When I come to the end of this challenge, what will be the benefits:

- To me?
- To others?
- When I come to the end of this challenge, what will be the costs
  - To me?
  - To others?
- Would I have the courage to pull out if my logical side was screaming 'Don't do it'?
- What is really going on? Be honest. What is driving me on at this point?
- What is the strength of my motivation on a scale of one to ten?

Chapter 6: CONNECT

Can you build a solid support network?

'*We don't accomplish anything in the world alone.*'

– Sandra Day O'Connor, first woman to become a
US Supreme Court Justice

While self-reliance is a vital quality in any adventurer, the willingness to draw on the strength of others is, arguably, even more important. That ability to connect is the focus of this chapter. It really is a crucial part of the process. Just as the right group of people bring the best out of each other, the wrong group – or even just one ill-chosen member – can jeopardise the enjoyment and success of an expedition. There are three critical elements to consider. First, how to get other people connected with your challenge. Second, how to decide if you should go solo or with a team. Third, if you do need a team, how to select them and get the best out of them.

Alone Or With Others?

In rare cases, people decide to go for something on their own, with no back-up. During the planning stage of my row across the Atlantic, I talked with someone who had completed the crossing about whether or not to go solo. He couldn't understand when I said I wanted to do it with someone else. He said: 'You need to know, John, that the biggest challenge is not the sharks (terrifying though they might look); it's not the waves (although, at 10 metres in height, they might scare the shit out of you); it's not the passing oil tankers (not even when they are heading towards you in the middle of the night and clearly don't know that you are in their path). No, John – none of that – it is the person in the boat with you: that is your biggest challenge. You wait, there will come a stage where you would love to kill him and he would love to kill you. The only thing stopping you both is the thought of being found out.'

Wow! Quite the warning. But even so, I decided that, given my strong extrovert personality type, I would crack up at sea if left on my own, so I sought out a rowing partner. However, my wife drew the line at inviting our 17-year-old son to row with me. 'I have to accept that you might well die on this venture,' she said, 'but you are not taking our son down with you.' Fortunately, Fraser Dodds, who had partnered me on many adventures, agreed to step up.

We had our testing moments, for sure, but we managed to avoid killing each other. And during the most challenging aspects of the row, I was glad to have Fraser with me. We made a great team – and I could not have done it without him.

If you have a burning ambition, you must decide whether you can, or will, go it alone. My experience has always led me to engage other people in support of what then becomes a shared endeavour. If you make that choice, you have to use all the skills at your disposal to make sure the people around you are as excited and energised by the challenge as you are. Anything less will be a drain on energy, time and resources, and the result will be failure and disappointment.

Look For Character Before Skills

If you choose to work with a team on your mission, don't be dazzled by ability. Skill can be developed, provided the basic building blocks are in place. Character is harder to create and harder to come by – but it is the thing that will keep someone moving forward when it is easier to give up. The key issue for me is to select a team that can cope with disaster and disappointment. And it is character, not skill, that can best help here.

The Perfect Team Leader In Action: Sir Ernest Shackleton

'Men Wanted for hazardous journey. Small wages, bitter cold, long months of complete darkness, constant danger, safe return doubtful. Honour and recognition in case of success.' – Sir Ernest Shackleton

Who would answer such an ad, which, the story goes, Shackleton placed in a London newspaper seeking men for his

1914 Imperial Trans-Antarctic Expedition? As it turns out, 27 of the toughest, most resilient explorers in history.

If you are to put your life on the line and, more importantly, be accountable for the lives of others, you have a responsibility to make sure the people coming with you fully understand the nature of the challenge and are committed to it.

If they are not in that frame of mind from the start, or if you feel they do not have the capacity to extend themselves far from their comfort zone, taking them with you is a bad idea.

My advice is to be like Shackleton: up front and honest about the risk and uncertainty to come, and then to be extremely careful about the sort of team you take with you. My experience has taught me to test the potential of the team members in situations or environments that approximate those of the expedition environment before setting off.

Selection For A Himalayan Team

In 1986, when recruiting a team to scale some unclimbed peaks in the Himalayas, I bore Shackleton's advert in mind. And just as he was inundated with responses, so was I. The severity of the ad's language had attracted certain people.

At an early stage in the selection process, I wrote to each interested person and reminded them that one in eight climbers died in the Himalayas on expedition. I told them it was important they told their partners and families the truth, as I was the one who would have to inform the bereaved families if their loved one did not return. That cut the numbers down a bit.

I then arranged a selection process in which people lived closely together and climbed together in groups for a week in the French Alps. At the end of that process, it was clear who would fit in and who wouldn't. The team decided that for themselves. However, there was one exception to this process: a work colleague of mine approached me a few months before we were due to leave England and suggested he should take on the role of base camp manager and photographer for the expedition. He would also film the expedition. The opportunity was too good to miss. He duly showed his commitment by filming while he trained.

However, he had not been on the training expedition with the rest of the team and so was unknown to them. He managed the base camp and filmed while I led the team up the mountain, but he was never fully accepted. He found himself in a terrible position in base camp – he simply could not win the hearts of the climbers. I vowed that never again would I take someone at the last minute to go on an expedition – however good their background and CV might look.

As Luck Would Have It

Psychologist Dr Richard Wiseman has conducted fascinating experiments with people who describe themselves as lucky or unlucky.[1] In one of them, an 'unlucky' person and a 'lucky' person were invited for separate interviews at a café. Wiseman also placed a £5 note on the front step of the café.

The 'unlucky' subject, nervously focused on the interview, did not notice the money as she entered. Wiseman, who let the subjects arrive before he did, had also ensured there was only one seat free in the café, next to a successful businessman. The unlucky subject sat next to him to wait, but did not say a word. When Wiseman later asked her about any lucky or unlucky events that day, she said it had been an uneventful morning.

The 'lucky' subject, on the other hand, pocketed the £5 note and struck up a conversation with the businessman while he waited. He told Wiseman he had found a fiver and had a very enjoyable chat.

The conclusion Wiseman drew is that you make your own luck. And part of that is in the networks you set up and your ability to connect. In other words, if you associate with people who often complain that life is unfair and who consider themselves to be unlucky, you too will be unlucky. But if you attach yourself to people who consider themselves lucky, there is every chance they will lift you up to share some of their luck.

Get a GRPI

Whether you are leading a business team or an expedition team, there are some key tasks you must take care of. I tend to rely on an old and well-tested model that was created by organisational theorist Richard Beckhard as a formula for developing high-performance teams. It's called GRPI.

Goals

Make sure that as a leader you have a clear idea where you are headed. You don't need all the details at this stage, but you must know where your true north is. I discussed this in chapter 5, Clarity.

This may shift as conditions change or you take advice from gifted colleagues, but you must be certain that any major change of direction is what you want and is in harmony with the pursuit of the primary goal.

In the early stages of an expedition, speak with individual team members about their hopes and fears. Some will want to see the team get to the summit – even if they are not selected to be in that final summit team. Others will care only about their own success. The time to sort this out is before departure, not in a fractious base-camp row at an altitude of 16,000 feet.

The same applies to your team at work. Good leaders will know the aspirations of their key team members and will do everything they can to help them achieve their goals.

Roles

Create clarity around people's roles and responsibilities, including your own. Be sure that every person who joins your team is happy to be led by you. If any of them have doubts, for reasons of jealousy, conflicting egos or anything else, address them immediately. If this does not work, do not take that person with you. I have turned many people away from my teams over the years, for various reasons. That said, there have also been people who had a shaky start but became great colleagues and team players.

Very often, you can avoid conflict and disharmony by being honest and assertive from the start. You also need to be clear about what you want from the team and – this is hugely important – understand what the team wants from you as their leader.

Processes

We have already spoken about the process of leadership in the team. What is the structure of leadership beneath you and – something that we were taught as young army officers – who would take over if anything happened to you? What is the chain of command?

Other things to consider: what is the decision-making process to be? Where does ultimate accountability lie? How much headroom does your team have regarding matters such as budgetary decisions? What processes are in place to enable conflict resolution?

This may sound like tedious stuff, but just like a lengthy partnership agreement drawn up by a solicitor, it will ensure smoother preparation and help keep you all safe if things go wrong.

Interpersonal relationships

Clashes among team members are almost inevitable. Sometimes these are the result of old conflicts that have never been properly resolved. Other times, it's a matter of jealousy over power and status or resource allocations. A lot of this can be resolved by some careful coaching and honest discussions with individuals, pairs or the team. This is the stock-in-trade of our management consultancy, Tiger Teams – helping people to have the discussions they are not confident enough to have by themselves.

In fairness, it is a lot easier for us as consultants to bring such discussions into the open, as we are not personally, psychologically or practically involved in the outcome. In the same way, it is sometimes easier for the leader to help resolve conflict issues between team members rather than let them struggle by themselves.

The worst thing the leader can do is to pretend these problems don't exist. That is a recipe for disaster.

Connecting With The Community

In 1986, when I returned from my Himalayan adventure, I found the police station in east London where I worked to be in a very vulnerable position. The officer in charge had experienced a nervous breakdown and I was told I would take over his job.

The local community was fragmented and conflict was not unusual. The one thing the people had in common was a dislike and distrust of the local police.

Some of the frontline police officers were scared, bruised and dispirited from their desperate efforts to try to bring down the level of street violence, robberies and open distribution of drugs. Many were cynical about attempts to bring peace to the streets, despite the committed and courageous work by community police officers to create trusted relationships in the area.

The local authority was somewhat hostile towards us, while the local schools banned us, lest we have a negative effect on their pupils. So, the challenges for me were:

1) What could I do to build trust in the local community so I could connect with them and truly be of service?

2) How could I connect with my frontline officers to win their support for a more neighbourhood-friendly policing strategy?

3) How could I find the leaders in the community with whom I could connect in a shared endeavour?

4) How could I do all this and win the support from a senior management team that was supervising us from a distant HQ?

5) What could I do to secure the funding required to put a strategy in place that would achieve our objectives?

While each of these challenges required its own approach, key to all of them was trust and communication – the crucial ingredients of connection.

The first thing I decided was that if I was to succeed – and within a short space of time – I would need to give all of my energy and commitment.

I would have to lead by example and let my values and my determination be clear to all of those for whom I was responsible, from my own officers to the people in the community who relied upon us for their personal safety.

I explained to my wife that I would rarely be at home for the next couple of years. I would often be required to work during the day and to go to evening meetings. I would be almost like an overseas missionary.

I had to decide (a) what I was trying to achieve, and (b) who I was working for. My answer to the first question was that I was working to achieve peace in a troubled area – anything less than that was off track. The second answer was that I would devote myself to being of service to the community. I had to find a way to connect with the different community groups in the area so that they trusted me to work with their interests in mind. To achieve this, I and my colleagues would need to set up meetings with local people and religious groups in the area.

The endeavour was tough and painful at times. On many occasions, I found myself standing alone as angry residents berated me about an experience they had had with one of my officers.

Gradually, however, the community grew to trust us more. And it was this trust that enabled me to defuse volatile situations that could easily have escalated into serious street violence.

All this could only be done through the concerted effort of police officers who had connected with the community on the ground. It was critical for everybody to understand that treating people with anything less than respect would not be tolerated.

So, what did I learn from this? Connection is vital to success for a leader who is charged with bringing people together and planning for a shared future. It is as simple and absolute as that.

Critical questions to ask yourself:

- Am I going to go it alone or do I need others to help?
- What are the key areas – of knowledge, skills and experience – in which I am lacking but can find in others?
- What critical conversations have I avoided but I know I need to have?
- Where am I going to find help?
- How can I attract the right people and maximise the potential benefit/support/resources they could bring to the project?
- How can I surround myself with the best possible people to improve the chances of success?
- Have I been clear about people's roles and responsibilities within the team, including my own?
- Have I ironed out any relationship issues between team members?
- Will I ask for help when it is needed?

Chapter 7: COURAGE

Do you have the resilience to stick at it?

'Life begins at the end of your comfort zone'

– Neale Donald Walsch, writer

Courage has been described as, among other things, 'the will to accomplish goals in the face of opposition or risk'[1] and 'perseverance despite fear'.[2] I think we all recognise courage when we see it in others and maybe, upon reflection, we can recall when we have shown courage ourselves – either by taking on a physical challenge or in simple choices we made in the moment, such as standing up to others. Courage plays a role in each of the previous critical Cs and is a key characteristic of any successful adventurer. In this chapter, my aim is to show you how to find, foster and harness the courage that lives inside you – so that you can call upon it when the situation demands.

The Negative Power Of Anxiety

Let us begin by looking at one of the common threats to courage: anxiety.

It is no surprise that anxiety – being uneasy or worried about what may happen – can negatively affect your courage. However, there are ways of reframing anxiety so you can better manage it. The social psychologist Geert Hofstede made a comparison between anxiety and fear, and uncertainty and risk, that I think is useful here:

'Uncertainty is to risk as anxiety is to fear. Fear and risk are both focused on something specific: an object in the case of fear, an event in the case of risk. Risk is often expressed as a percentage of probability that a particular event may happen. Anxiety and uncertainty are both diffuse feelings.[3]

Anxiety, then, has no object. Likewise, uncertainty has no probability attached to it. As soon as uncertainty is expressed as risk, however, it ceases to be a source of anxiety. It may become a source of fear, but it may also be accepted as routine – like the risks of driving a powerful car or routinely engaging in a sport such as rock climbing or skydiving.

In looking at the relationship between anxiety and fear, the suggestion is that anxiety is unhealthy, whereas fear can be healthy. In other words, fear with an object can fulfil a useful function, as opposed to anxiety, which generally brings with it an all-pervasive feeling that leaves you weak and impotent.

The trick is to change uncertainty to risk by analysing what you are worried about, using a left-brain risk-assessment process.

When working with individuals as a personal coach, one of my greatest thrills comes from breaking through the uncertainty barrier and beginning scenario planning and risk analysis. If you can face up to risk in its real state, you are far better able to manage it than when you are feeling anxious regarding the uncertainty of what might lie ahead.

The 'Fear Bubble' Technique

Another useful tool for quelling anxiety is what former Royal Marine Ant Middleton calls the Fear Bubble technique.[4] It suggests that you don't have to worry about the thing that is making you scared until you get to that point (eg, an interview). You compartmentalise and keep the fear bound to a certain point in the future, inside a bubble. The rest of the time, you concentrate on staying calm and doing what you can to equip yourself for the moment of challenge. When the moment comes, you step into the bubble.

For example, on many major climbs, there is often one awkward move that is mission critical – the one move that poses the greatest threat to your safety and your life. As important as this moment is, you don't want to spend the whole climb worrying about it. Doing so will take up your energy and strength, leaving you in a terrified and weakened state when the moment comes. It is necessary to feel the fear and grind your way through it when you get to that point – but not before. I am not talking about reckless abandon here or denial, but mind control. This notion has kept me alive on many tricky occasions and I have recommended Middleton's Fear Bubble to many others to help them manage anxiety. You don't need to lapse into fight-or-flight mode; just concentrate on controlling the controllable.

Fear Of Failure

Recently, a global finance consultancy conducted a survey of one thousand of the company's executives, from management trainees to board directors. The survey found that the majority of these key individuals were more likely to be afraid of failure than to be excited by challenge. Fifty-seven per cent of respondents admitted to backing away from, rather than embracing, new challenges as they moved up the career ladder. The resulting report found that a lack of confidence, not a lack of ability, was holding people back.

But what holds people back from their potential to display courage when faced with uncomfortable levels of risk? As described in the Capable chapter, each of us has a different natural psychological appetite for risk in different aspects of our lives. Indeed, I use questionnaires to measure this when I am coaching clients. If we allow our brain free rein, we should be able to conquer these natural fears.

But what goes on in our brains to hold us back from taking the risks that part of us is desperate to take? What creates a fear so powerful that it overwhelms a desire to take on a challenge?

Chimp, Human And Computer

To better handle fear, it pays to know a little about how the human brain works. In his book *The Chimp Paradox*,[5] psychiatrist Professor Steve Peters explains the crucial role the reptilian brain plays in alerting us to imminent danger. It is the part of the brain that causes animals and humans to fight, take flight or freeze when they sense danger.

Peters calls this part of the brain the Chimp. The influence of the Chimp is very powerful and can easily overpower the slower moving, more rational and analytical part of the brain, which he calls the Human. In short, our Chimp brain can fire up unnecessarily at times and, in its efforts to protect us, it can prevent us from taking risks that might well benefit us.

Both the Human brain and the Chimp brain reach into the third metaphorical part of the brain, which Peters calls the Computer. This stores experiences, good and bad, for the Chimp and the Human to draw on when making decisions around risk. If the Chimp detects a pattern of potential extreme misadventure in the Computer storage, it will guide us away from risk.

The information stored in the Computer brain determines our capacity to take on (and, perhaps, relish) extreme risks in uncertain situations. For some of us, the constant widening of our experience of risky ventures will lead to a store of images pointing to future possibility rather than fearful risk to be avoided.

The Courage To Be Happy

It is, of course, easier to continue living in your comfort zone, believing perhaps that much of your life remains outside your control, or that certain things are beyond your ability. In *The Courage to be Disliked*,[6] authors Ichiro Kishimi and Fumitake Koga use the theories of Alfred Adler – founder of the school of individual psychology – to illustrate what keeps people locked into a limited existence:

'You could say that it is like driving your familiar old car. It might rattle a bit, but one can take that into account and manoeuvre easily. On the other hand, if one chooses a new lifestyle, no one can predict what might happen to the new self or have any idea how to deal with events as they arise.

'When we try to change our lifestyles, we put our great courage to the test ... Adlerian psychology is a psychology of courage. Your unhappiness cannot be blamed on your past or environment. And it isn't that you lack competence. You just lack courage. One might say you are lacking the courage to be happy.'

It's worth asking whether you're letting past events keep you in a comfort zone. Are you blaming them for your current unhappiness? And, crucially, is it a lack of competence or a lack of courage that's been holding you back? Or is it that pesky chimp chattering in your ear at night, reminding you that this crazy adventure of yours is, potentially, extremely dangerous?

Fear Of Success

In many ways, the fear of success sounds nonsensical. After all, how can anybody feel frightened of success? But in a strange way, it fills us with a sense of foreboding that is just as powerful as the fear of failure.

Some years ago, I was considering starting a new business. In preparation for the launch, I had a strategic workshop with the colleagues who would be working with me. I also engaged the services of a management consultant to talk to us as part of the planning process.

One of the questions he asked was, 'What would happen in three years' time if you became very successful?' To my surprise, I was filled with a sense of dread. What would this mean to me? It would surely involve a position similar to my former role as a police divisional commander, where I had responsibility for hundreds of people. If 'successful', I would return to the world of HR departments, sales departments and marketing departments. I would have spreadsheets of endless figures and be tied to an office.

The consultant asked me why I found this question so troubling. I explained my predicament and he said, 'Is that, then, how you define success?' I remember replying to him, 'Well, it must be like this, surely? If you're successful, you have to have an empire, loads of staff and all the problems that go with it.'

'Does it really?' he asked. 'When you are working and you are at your happiest, describe it to me.' I explained my work at our farm in the Lake District, in Cumbria; it's way off the beaten track, in the most stunning surroundings and without another house in view. That is where I run leadership programmes. I described the intense feeling of satisfaction when I see people grow and develop in that environment. I feel privileged to witness such moments; indeed, on many occasions, I have said to my colleagues something like, 'Do you know, the experience is so fantastic that I would do this for nothing – in fact, I'd even pay to do it!'

The consultant said, 'If this is how you define success, why don't you design yourself a life where you are doing nothing else but this?'

When he said that, I remember thinking that would be fantastic. Such a goal would certainly be sufficient to get me out of bed in the morning; more than that, it would offer me a feeling of immense satisfaction and pride. Consequently, it is to this that I have dedicated my life over the last seven years. We must each define success in a way that speaks to us personally and not necessarily how others see it.

The challenge that faces us all, therefore, is to work out for ourselves what success will look like – and then have the courage to pursue it.

Talent Needs Trauma

Self-help author Napoleon Hill believed this point of confrontation and challenge was crucial to success. For his studies of rich, very successful Americans from the 1930s to the 1950s, he would ask them to describe pivotal moments where a problem seemed insurmountable. Gradually, they would haul themselves over the hurdle and make their way forward to success. Hill was convinced that no serious advance could occur without such challenges. This is similar to the notion that talent needs trauma – to succeed you must have built strength and resilience by overcoming significant hurdles. Certainly, when you look at the backstories of many successful sportspeople, businesspeople or artists, they have often had to overcome major difficulties. Courage comes from the knowledge they can – and have – overcome challenges. Now – think about a time when *you've* shown courage.

Self-limiting Beliefs

Motivational speaker and self-help author Tony Robbins has written a great deal about self-limiting beliefs, or what have also been described as gremlins – those mischievous little figures that sit on our shoulders, haunting us, reminding us of the things we find hard to do and trying to convince us we are not good enough to succeed.

In some cases, these are messages we pick up in early childhood and they stay with us forever. Sadly, all too often, offhand comments from parents or siblings reduce us to a lesser state.

While these gremlins may never truly leave us, we can certainly learn to recognise, understand and – if our courage is well developed – master them.

All At Sea

In September 1975, some work colleagues and I set out to cross the Channel in a small chartered boat. We reached Cherbourg successfully but, on the return journey, ran into a force 10 gale.

The captain struggled to hold things together, but one crew member had been a second mate in the merchant navy and his skills as a navigator were extraordinary. At the height of the storm, he managed to take sextant readings that provided us with a pinpoint-accurate position and so he was able to navigate us towards the Needles Lighthouse, on the Isle of Wight.

At this point the wind was cyclonic – which means that it whipped around in vicious circles – rendering it impossible for us to set a straight course, so we began to veer towards the red zone of the lighthouse, perilously close to the rocks.

We fought to turn the boat around, which we finally accomplished with interest – we were catapulted back out to sea by the strong wind and huge waves.

We tried to get the mainsail down but each time we had an armful, it would try to throw us overboard. Eventually, we managed to lash it down, but the foresail had become knotted onto the guard rails at the front of the boat and was impossible to reach.

We knew we were in trouble and fired off a distress rocket, which was answered immediately from land. Fortunately, HM Coastguard had been watching our progress and had us in their sights. The Yarmouth lifeboat was launched and set off through the horrendous seas to attempt a rescue. But the lifeboat was battered by the huge waves to such an extent that the crew lost the use of their radar, so they had to call on the help of a Royal Navy vessel to get an exact fix on their location.

Gradually, the two boats moved closer and, in the early hours of the morning, they finally pulled alongside us in 30-foot waves. The coxswain shouted through a loudhailer that they could neither take us in tow, nor get a breeches buoy to us to winch us from our boat to the lifeboat. Our only hope was to jump from the boat onto the lifeboat.

At this stage, the skipper handed control of the boat to me. I was the least experienced crew member aboard, but I managed to keep the two boats from smashing together. Our skipper was the first to jump and he was quickly followed by the rest of the crew – I was left in maddening chaos, still attempting to steer the boat.

I turned and climbed onto the guard rails before jumping into the white of the lights and the spray. I distinctly remember clinging to the rails and the side of the boat before the crew members picked me up and threw me onto the deck of the lifeboat.

Our boat was left to its own devices as we set off, struggling to turn into the winds and the waves to make our way back to safety. Many people on that lifeboat were struggling with sea sickness and wondering if we would ever return alive. We had assumed we were safe once we reached the lifeboat but later discovered this was a terrifying experience for our rescuers, too. Finally, at 4am, we made it to safety on the Isle of Wight.

Sometime later, the crew of the lifeboat came to London to receive an award for their gallantry. We took them to dinner, which was the least we could do for people who had risked their lives for us.

Year later, when I first considered the possibility of rowing across the Atlantic, I was asked many times, 'Do you realise you will have to face 30-foot waves and horrendous seas behind your boat for much of the time?' I remember thinking that I'd survived as much during my first trip to sea in a sailing boat, and it hadn't felt that bad. This was ignorance on my part, as I knew little of the skills needed for sailing, but, nevertheless, my boundaries had been pushed further than most people would ever experience and the thought of extending them again seemed plausible. I had faced my fear, managed it and felt able to do so again. So, maybe for each of us, the challenge is to keep stretching the boundaries of possibilities in various facets of our lives. These stretch experiences will instil the courage to face any challenge.

Critical questions to ask yourself:

- When am I at my most courageous?
- What could I do to become more courageous?
- Is my Chimp brain making too many of the decisions?
- How will I find the courage to make my dream a reality?
- Do I fear success as well as failure?
- What are my self-limiting beliefs?

Conclusion

How to take on your next challenge

As you reach the end of this book, I hope it has inspired you to seek out exciting, challenging, life-affirming journeys.

Some of you will have already set out on challenges far more serious in nature than I have experienced. For others, these adventures are yet to come. Whatever the case, I commend the model of the Seven Cs as a guide for your next challenge.

At times, the journey may not be comfortable; neither will it necessarily make you popular with those who care about you. However, it may make you a more interesting, more curious and more capable person.

It's impossible to know what challenges lie in wait. But if you can face them with confidence and courage, you'll have a better chance of coping with whatever life throws at you.

My hope is that some of the thoughts in this book will sustain you on that life adventure. Your future is in your hands.

Appendix

Coping Strategies

During an adventure, your ability to cope with challenging situations will be tested, so you will need to be as mentally strong as you are physically fit. I wanted to dedicate part of the book to this key area.

The stress container

During the coronavirus lockdowns, I coached quite a few people who were struggling to stay positive. These were people I would rate as strong life performers, but many felt things were falling apart and their sense of capability and self-belief was in tatters.

At the time, I was doing an online mental health first aid course run by Mental Health First Aid that had a useful model to describe how rational and competent people can find themselves in this position. It's called The Stress Container. The idea is that all of us have a notional stress container into which we put items in our life that take up our energy and can potentially cause us stress, such as work challenges and financial worries. Eventually, the container fills up and starts to overflow. As the container overflows we may develop a series of negative behaviours – including 'faulty thinking'.

Stress Container Model

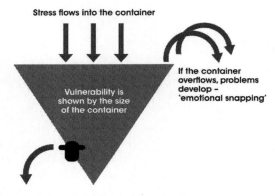

Stress flows into the container

Vulnerability is shown by the size of the container

If the container overflows, problems develop – 'emotional snapping'

Helpful coping strategies = a working tap lets the stress out
Unhelpful coping strategies = the tap becomes blocked, so water fills the container and overflows

Image: Mental Health First Aid England
mhfaengland.org

What regulates the process?

The key issue is the size of our container. If we have a large container, we can afford to take on many stressors. If our container is small, we are likely to run into difficulty. In this book I have discussed the need to expand our potential by taking on stretch challenges. If we can do this, the size of our container will increase. If we take on too much, however, we will become overwhelmed and the container becomes smaller.

An important aspect of this model is the tap at the bottom of the container, which can be opened to relieve pressure. To do this, we need positive coping strategies. These include going for a walk, reading, socialising, sharing feelings, eating well and getting enough sleep. Any one of these could help bring down the level in our container.

However, we should be wary of unhealthy coping strategies – overreacting in the moment, overeating or not eating enough, drinking too much alcohol or coffee, smoking, taking drugs, withdrawing from friends and those who could help us, bottling up feelings and overworking. These unhealthy coping strategies do not turn on the release tap. They just block it and exacerbate our problems.

It is not the purpose of this book to lecture on stress management, but I wanted to remind you that, as an adventurer, you need to (a) increase the size of your stress container if you are going to take on serious challenges and (b) build up a portfolio of useful coping strategies that will keep you afloat when times are tough.

Bangor University's Institute for the Psychology of Elite Performance has conducted some good research on coping strategies.[1] You will almost certainly spot techniques you are already using. You will also probably recognise some coping strategies that you are overusing or neglecting – and one or two that should be removed from your toolbox.

Stress And Coping

Primary and secondary appraisal

A hugely influential theory of stress and coping was developed in 1984 by psychologists Richard Lazarus and Susan Folkman, who defined coping as a process of 'constantly changing cognitive and behavioural efforts to manage specific external and/or internal demands or conflicts that are appraised as taxing or exceeding one's resources'.

The essence of this definition is that coping is a dynamic sequence of steps and not a static state. Coping strategies appear in two ways. First, your primary appraisal. In other words, 'What is happening? What is at stake for me in this encounter?'

You then move on to what is known as secondary appraisal: 'What can I do about the stress?' or 'Do I have the ability to manage this?'

The way we approach the different coping strategies changes as the encounter unfolds – and, indeed, as we move from encounter to encounter. We use a range of coping strategies to deal with different stress sources, but we tend to have favourites. Under stress, we rely on techniques with which we are most comfortable.

Elite performers use multiple strategies – often simultaneously and in combination with one another. The strategies used by the most successful athletes or performers are so deeply ingrained that they become automatic. But everyone can be taught to cope more effectively with stress by developing a wider range of coping strategies.

There are four key sets of coping strategies:

- Problem focused
- Emotion focused
- Avoidance
- Appraisal – reappraisal (reframing)

Each of these key sets can be broken down into four subsets.

Problem Focused

These are the practical efforts we make to manage the problem that is causing us stress, or try to alter the source of that stress. This involves gathering information and dealing with the situation using rational thinking and problem-solving techniques.

Problem-focused coping strategies can be relied upon when situations are amenable to change and where you have control over the important elements of the stressful encounter (you can do something about what is causing the stress.)

Typical problem-solving strategies will be actions you take to address the problem – ie, planning, prioritising, showing restraint, holding back on other distracting activities and seeking technical advice.

Problem-focused strategies:

<u>Active coping</u>

This is the process whereby we take steps to tackle the stressor that is troubling us. It includes initiating direct action and trying to execute coping in a sequential and ordered fashion.

The drive for me during the worst of the coronavirus pandemic was to make sure that at the end of each day I would be able to tick off certain things I had achieved that day. This could be anything from a run in the nearby forest, tidying up parts of the house that rarely got attention, decorating, repairing things and even writing a few pages of this book. It felt crucial to have a pattern for the day – some sort of routine with a sense of purpose.

When I was rowing across the ocean, I used to spend at least one of my off-duty two-hour sessions checking the mechanical parts of the boat – the rudder mechanism, the fresh-water maker, the electrics etc. Anything to make the day go by with a sense of some achievement other than monotonously sliding back and forth on a rowing machine – making incredibly slow progress and seemingly going nowhere.

<u>Restraint</u>

This is the process of forcing ourselves to hold back. It may involve blanking out the pressure from those who are desperate for us to take immediate action. In short, it involves staying cool and choosing tactics only after weighing them up carefully. It is an active strategy, not avoidance, because it involves a focused and deliberate attempt to deal with the stressor. But it is also a passive activity in the sense that using restraint means not acting.

This is almost the opposite of active coping. For example, during the lockdowns, we refrained from going out and doing things that were unnecessary, to avoid catching or spreading the virus. We had to stay indoors, not see people, not make unnecessary journeys etc – a hard thing for someone who wrote a book called *Restless*.

Suppression of competing activities

This means putting other projects aside and screening out distractions. It may involve deliberately letting other things slide to deal with a stressor. The key activity here is prioritisation and to focus on the immediate challenge or threat in hand.

Planning

This involves coming up with strategies for action and thinking about the best ways to handle a problem. It is quite different from active coping in that it is focused on systematically thinking about the problem rather than lurching into doing something.

Emotion Focused

These are the strategies we use for reducing or managing the emotional distress that results from the problem associated with (or caused by) the situation in which we find ourselves. They are cognitive efforts to change the 'meaning' but not the actual problem or the environment of the situation.

Problem-focused and emotion-focused coping strategies have very different roots.

'Problem-focused coping tends to predominate when people feel that something constructive can be done, whereas emotion-focused coping tends to predominate when people feel that the stressor is something that must be endured.'[2]

Emotion-focused strategies can thus be relied upon when situations are not amenable to change and where you have little control over the situation and the recurrence of stress.

These are the cases where you realise that everything you had planned has gone awry, but you have to endure not only the pain of the moment but a considerable amount of pain to come.

It's what I call being able to keep your head together when you have no idea what's going to happen next and how you will react. All you know is that if you keep cool you will – somehow – find your way out of the situation.

Typically, emotion-focused coping strategies include seeking support or taking advice from others to help deal with your emotions and prevent you from feeling overwhelmed. Some may find solace in their religion or some other spiritual source.

Emotion-focused strategies also include having the courage to vent your feelings rather than bottling them up. A remarkable number of seasoned ocean rowers have stunned their rowing partners by suddenly collapsing into despair and abandoning the endeavour. They had felt unable to vent and share their feelings until it was too late. Their rowing partners had no idea what was going on inside.

Part of the research conducted by sports psychologists during a transatlantic rowing event 10 years ago focused on people's capacity to get in touch with their emotions. Based on earlier studies, the researchers predicted that the ability of the rowers to embrace their feelings would increase as the event progressed. By the end of the event, they would be much more able to talk about and express their emotions and have deeper feelings towards their partners back home. This is exactly what happened.

I have witnessed great emotional changes in clients who are faced with life-threatening situations in remote parts of the world. They find they can talk profoundly about their emotions and share them with their partners on a satellite phone. I once received a text from a client who had phoned his partner from the Namibian desert because he suddenly realised how much she meant to him. When he returned to the UK, they got married. His text included a photograph of their first child.

There have been occasions where rowers have staggered off their boats after crossing 3,000 miles of the Atlantic Ocean, dropped to their knees and asked their partner to marry them. You would have thought they would be mentally hardened by their gruelling experience, but often it has brought out the softer side of their personality. Perhaps it was all those silent, singular moments, where the majesty of the sky and expanse of the ocean allowed them to think differently and to focus on what was truly important in life.

Emotion-focused strategies:

Focus on venting of emotions

This is when you focus on whatever is upsetting you so you can vent your feelings. There is evidence that focusing on such emotions for long periods can hold back adjustment. It may distract people from getting on and engaging in active efforts to move beyond the distress. However, like every coping strategy, there is a place for it.

The classic example is a period of mourning to come to terms with the loss of a loved one – or even a dream or opportunity – so you can move forward.

On a practical level, I've heard ocean rowers talk about screaming for 45 seconds when they sat down at the start of their two-hour stint, to help them cope with the pain to come. It helped them endure the moment and move on into action.

Use of instrumental social support

This is when you seek advice, assistance or information. Although this falls under the banner of emotion-focused rather than problem-focused strategies, the distinction is debatable.

On an event such as rowing the Atlantic, problem-focused strategies and quick thinking will help you to survive. Making decisions under pressure is a skill that will be the difference between success and failure, or life and death.

The problem for an endurance adventurer is that you become very tired. Your mind becomes less able to respond intelligently to problems. This is when faulty thinking occurs.

During the 10-week Atlantic crossing, I was fortunate that my wife, Elaine, was able to talk to me on a fairly regular basis – typically once every two days – and to sanity check some of the decisions we were trying to grapple with out there. There were times when I was so tired and confused that I would have found it impossible even to spell my name. Without the regular input of emotional support from Elaine, I would have been truly sunk.

Use of emotional social support

This is the process of seeking out and using moral support, sympathy and understanding. Very often this will occur in tandem with social support, but it is different. This category can be a lifesaver for those in extremely dangerous and stressful situations – long live the satellite phone. However, it is important that you do not overuse this strategy. On the one hand, when you are struggling with anxiety and feelings of insecurity, such reassurance from someone outside your situation can be immensely powerful. On the other hand, it can lead to a sense of learnt helplessness or projection onto the helper in a way that could become dysfunctional if relied upon too often.

Spiritual coping

A cynic might say that turning to religion for support in a time of extreme crisis or stress could be classified as avoidance coping. However, whatever works for you is what matters.

I suspect there are very few ocean rowers who have not had some kind of spiritual experience, however brief, that helped them when things were particularly tough. Certainly, after times of extreme personal danger, I have enjoyed spiritual moments that helped me return to safety.

Avoidance

These are the efforts we make to physically or mentally disengage from the stressful situation. They can manifest as a tendency to avoid or ignore the threat, or external information.

This approach includes focusing on something (often work) to take your mind off the problem, watching TV or even sleeping. It could also involve denial – pretending the situation does not exist. Avoidance can also involve simply throwing in the towel and giving up – convincing yourself that it has become impossible to address the situation. And, of course, one of the most common forms of avoidance is to turn to alcohol or drugs to dim the pain of reality.

Avoidance can be an effective strategy in the short term, as a situation could change. It can be used to reduce short-term anxiety and worry that can distract from your performance. This is the pretense that everything is going to be fine, despite the fact there is no evidence to suggest this will be the case.

This attitude was typified by my reaction when I was trapped in a storm for several days on the summit of Peak 6529 in the Himalayas. My instinct was to try to convince the people around me that the weather was getting better, despite the lack of evidence. It may have given my colleagues some encouragement in the short term – and the weather did finally improve. Of course, this kind of avoidance is a pitiful strategy in the long term – particularly when it becomes clear that nothing is changing.

Facing up to reality is hard in dangerous and highly pressurised situations. Very often, all that is required is a switch to one of the other strategies to winch yourself into a different mindset.

Avoidance coping strategies:

Behavioural disengagement

This is where you reduce the effort you are putting into dealing with the stressor and even – at its extreme – just giving up on your attempt to achieve your goals. It may seem a sure path to despair but in situations where other coping mechanisms do not seem useful, it can be entirely appropriate. For example, if you are confronted by a mugger on a dark street at night, giving up the thought of fighting to save your wallet may be entirely sensible.

In 2009, I walked away in the early stages of an extreme ultramarathon in Namibia because I knew the fierce heat would be too much for me. It turned out to be one of the best decisions I have ever made – six hours later I saw other participants hooked up to drips and urinating blood.

I looked at the range of coping strategies available to me and decided that, for once in my life, tactical withdrawal was the best option. I returned the following year, much better prepared, and finished the race.

Mental disengagement

This is used in situations when conditions prevent you from behavioural disengagement. In other words, you have no option but to hang on and survive the drama you are facing.

The skill here is to distract yourself from thinking about the situation or the goal that the stressor is threatening. You have to find ways to switch to alternative activities to take your mind off a problem. Typical activities for most people would be daydreaming, escaping through sleep, or immersion in websites, computer games, TV or music.

In the Atlantic I would have gone mad with boredom or anxiety if I had not been able to use this strategy effectively. I used music a lot to escape from the moment. I also used to imagine that I was going for a one-hour run in the forest near my home. In my mind I would pound out every step of the way at different times of the year, and relive the smells and views that were so different from the endless vista of an ocean that felt like a prison.

Denial

Denial is a sorry option, as it usually ends in tears when the waves of reality eventually crash into you. However, it can buy you time in the short term. It might just allow you enough confidence, temporarily, to overcome your fears and face the moment with a sense of hope, when you have no strategy in mind to deal with the issue that challenges you.

Substance use

This is a familiar strategy. Many of us reach for a gin and tonic to wipe away the pressures and worries of the day. But the benefits are short-lived. We took three bottles of whisky on our ocean rowing boat and never touched a drop – it seemed ridiculously inappropriate. However, the most precious medicine for us on the trip turned out to be diazepam, which was a lifesaver when our spirits were down.

Depression is the ocean rower's best-kept secret and it's hard to handle on your own. Anything goes to help you escape its clutches. I have heard of rowers drifting for days as they tried to overcome a bout of depression. Prevention is ten times better than cure and, in my view, any strategy goes when your survival is at stake.

Appraisal/Reappraisal

These strategies involve efforts to appraise or reappraise the stressful situation. This is about changing perception rather than reality. It's sometimes referred to as 'reframing' or 'cognitive redefinition'. In its simplest terms, it's looking at things differently.

Appraisal/reappraisal coping strategies:

Positive reinterpretation and growth

This can sometimes just require the courage to look at things in a more positive light – trying to see the good in a situation. (Be careful you don't make things worse for a colleague working through depression.)

The trick here is to encourage thoughts such as, 'Well, I learnt something there – I won't make that mistake again'; 'One day, when I get out of here, I will be a whole lot wiser and a better person'; or 'Each mistake is a great opportunity for learning about what I am engaged in and about myself.'

In my opinion, by the time you have reached this phase, you have passed the avoidance stage and are coming to terms with reality in a more philosophical way. You are starting to think 'OK, so I can't change what has happened, so what can I learn from or get out of this situation?' Learning to live with the new reality and facing it in a new way can be hugely empowering.

Challenge

This is when you see the situation as an exciting challenge and get on with things. You can look at the beauty around you and remind yourself why you are doing what you are doing and that it will all be worthwhile in the end.

Humour

Reappraisal coping also includes humour – the ability to laugh at the craziness of the situation you find yourself in. When Fraser and I were enduring the daily grind of rowing across the ocean, the one thing that would make our day was when the other rower banged his head while climbing out of the cabin. Every time it happened, the rower would almost fall out of his seat in tears of laughter and this invariably set off the hapless victim, too. Humour can be a real tonic when times are hard and is a common strategy among people enduring great hardship.

Acceptance

Sometimes, it is a matter of accepting that the events are simply part of the challenge. You just have to deal with them.

I tend to get to a point where I see the day as my job. For the next few days or the next few weeks, my job is to run across the desert or to row across the ocean. Nothing more is required of me during that time – pretty straightforward living, really.

When I was rowing in bad weather, I used to compare myself with a trawlerman in the North Sea who goes out in foul weather to drag in nets in the dark. I only had to put up with discomfort for a few weeks before returning to a warm office for the rest of my working life. That put things in perspective for me.

The appraisal/reappraisal strategy is, to my mind, one of the most effective. It is about coming to terms with the fact that reality has changed and to stop trying to hold on to what you had planned to do or hoped was going to happen.

It's about being able to turn the situation on its head and find a solution – to think outside the box. It is also the capacity to draw success from what would appear to be a failure. Something has gone wrong and you are thinking of it as a learning opportunity. By doing this you will be able to deal with similar crises in the future.

The goal is to broaden your repertoire of coping-strategy options and then to strategically choose which one (or which blend) to use for each occasion.

The first step is to separate the strategies you use most often from those you rarely choose. From there, you can decide which ones you need to practise to build up your armoury. This understanding has hugely improved my capacity to take on seemingly impossible challenges and come out of them sane and in one piece – and sometimes a little wiser, too, I hope.

References

Chapter 2: Capable

1. Heidi Grant Halvorson, *Succeed: How We Can Reach Our Goals*, Prune, 2012.
2. Charles Blackmore, *Conquering the Desert of Death: Across the Taklamakan,* I.B. Tauris, 2007.
3. Colin Mortlock, *The Adventure Alternative*, Cicerone Press, 2nd edition, 1998.
4. Stephen R Covey, *The 7 Habits of Highly Effective People,* Simon & Schuster, 1989.

Chapter 3: Curiosity

1. Todd Kashdan, *Curious? Discover the Missing Ingredient to a Fulfilling Life,* Harper Perennial; reprint edition, 2013.
2. Carol S. Dweck, *Mindset: the New Psychology of Success*, Ballantine Books; reprint edition, 2007.
3. Carlos Castaneda, *Journey to Ixtlan*, Simon & Schuster, 1972.

Chapter 4: Commit

1. Bob Goldman, *Death in the Locker Room: Steroids and Sports*, Icarus Pr, 1984.
2. Napoleon Hill, *Think and Grow Rich*, Capstone, 2009.
3. Dr Scott Stanley, *Sliding vs Deciding: Cohabitation, Relationship Development and Commitment,* https://www.youtube.com/watch?v=5TpuIWdy6aE

4. Melissa L. Kamins and Carol S. Dweck, *Person Versus Process Praise and Criticism: Implications for Contingent Self-Worth and Coping,* Developmental Psychology, 1999, vol. 35, No.3, 835-847.

5. *When Goals are Known: the Effects of Audience Relative Status on Goal Commitment and Performance*, Journal of Applied Psychology, April 2020, 105(4), 372-389.

6. Sarah Gardner and Dave Albee, *Study Focuses on Strategies for Achieving Goals, Resolutions,* https://scholar.dominican. edu/news-releases/266/

Chapter 5: Clarity

1. Angela Duckworth, *GRIT: Why Passion and Resilience are the Secrets to Success,* Vermilion, 2017.

Chapter 6: Connect

1. Dr Richard Wiseman, *The Luck Factor: the Scientific Study of the Lucky Mind,* Arrow, 2004.

Chapter 7: Courage

1. Peterson & Seligman, 2004.

2. Rachman, 1990.

3. Geert Hofstede, Gert Jan Hofstede & Michael Minkov, *Cultures and Organizations: Software of the Mind,* McGraw Hill; third edition, 2010.

4. Ant Middleton, *The Fear Bubble: Harness Fear and Live Without Limits*, HarperCollins, 2020

5. Prof. Steve Peters, *The Chimp Paradox: the Mind Management Programme for Confidence, Success and Happiness*, Vermilion, 2012.

6. Ichiro Kishimi and Fumitake Koga, *The Courage to be Disliked: How to Free Yourself, Change Your Life and Achieve Real Happiness*, Allen & Unwin, 2019.

Appendix

1. Lew Hardy, Graham Jones and Daniel Gould, *Understanding Psychological Preparation for Sport: Theory and Practice of Elite Performers*, John Wiley & Sons, 1996.
2. Folkman & Lazarus, 1980.

Acknowledgements

Since writing my first book, *Restless*, a few years ago, I have struggled many times with the question, 'How do you get an idea in your head to do something seemingly impossible and bring it to the point of completion?' This book is my attempt at an answer.

Fortunately, I've not taken on this quest alone. I received support from writers whose editing skills are far better than mine.

My companion for the early part of this journey was my good friend George Bull, who shares my love of adventure and is a master of resilience. The hours we spent together discussing the model that became the Seven Cs were magical, and his enthusiasm and energy were a tonic and an inspiration to me on my writing adventure.

George's good chum, running partner and fellow editor, Rick Pearson, then took the baton and helped bring the book to the next stage of development. Rick had the courage to take out a red pen and hone the content, before handing it to the final editor – John Carroll – to bring out the surgeon's knife. John reminded me of my supervisor when I was writing up my dissertation for a master's degree late in life. He was ruthless in testing my assumptions and forced me to seriously engage the left side of my brain. I hope that with John's help I have acknowledged in these pages all the writers who have inspired and influenced my thinking throughout my life and who helped to form my ideas. Please forgive me if I have inadvertently failed to acknowledge someone. That is the last thing I would have wanted.

The icing on the cake was the work done by Ken Dawson, who designed the cover. Thanks for your patience and creativity, Ken.

Together, George, Rick, John, Ken and myself have made a very good team in bringing this book to fruition, and I am grateful to them for all they have done to make it possible.

Thanks also to Professor Tim Woodman from the Institute for the Psychology of Elite Performance at Bangor University, for giving me permission to use the material on Coping Strategies in the final chapter. And I'm also grateful to Professor Lew Hardy, formerly of Bangor University, for introducing me to the topic at a time when I needed it most.

To the many audiences who have shared my stories in talks over the years, and whose enthusiasm and engagement with elements of those stories helped me pull the Seven Cs model into place, I thank you. It is for you – and others like you – that I share this book, with the deep desire to help you move to the next stage of your journey.

Most importantly, my thanks go to my wife, Elaine, who has patiently endured many hours of me writing in our caravan in Devon by the sea. I will be forever grateful to Elaine and my boys for their forbearance and generosity over the years, when I was disappearing time and again to far-flung corners of the world, testing myself and putting the Seven Cs model into practice.

Finally, thanks to you – the reader – for coming with me on this journey. I will be so happy if this book opens a previously closed door – perhaps to a challenge that has been waiting for you for a long time.

The Author

John Peck is a former 2nd Lieutenant in the 1st Battalion, The Staffordshire Regiment. After he left the army, he joined the Metropolitan Police as a constable, patrolling the streets of London. In the mid-1980s, he commanded a police division in Stoke Newington, then an often-dangerous part of the city and a place where relations between the police and the community had reached their lowest ebb.

He has always pushed himself to the limits to do extraordinary things. In 1966, while in the army, he and a young officer climbed Popocatépetl, an active volcano and Mexico's second-highest peak. In 1986, he led a British/Indian police expedition to summit unclimbed mountains in the Himalayas. He learnt much about leading people during this period and was invited to run leadership-development programmes for senior police officers at the national Police Staff College in Hampshire.

In 1995, at the age of 50 and feeling restless, he left the police to set up a consultancy, training business leaders in the private sector.

In 2004, John became the oldest British person to row across the Atlantic Ocean unsupported and he spent the next decade continuing to find out how his body and mind would cope in extreme situations, from desert marathons to walking to the North Pole.

John now splits his time between coaching senior business leaders and their teams, through his consultancy Tiger Teams – tigerteams.co.uk – and running leadership challenge events in remote parts of the UK for inner city charities. He is well known for his powerful talks, in which he inspires people to take on challenges that may at first seem impossible – a subject that is dear to his heart and the focus of this book.

He does much of this work with his wife, Elaine, and his three sons – all of whom have been on expeditions with him over the years. He lives near Epping, Essex, and, when not working, he is often to be seen trudging up and down the muddy hills of Epping Forest with 20 kilos on his back.

If you are interested in exploring the Seven Cs model for your personal development or to find out how you can use the model in your business, please visit **seven-cs.co.uk**

Printed in Great Britain
by Amazon

14588930R00075